The Surprise of the Sacred

Peter Millar, who was formerly Warden of Iona Abbey, is a minister of the Church of Scotland and a member of the Iona Community. He and his late wife, Dr Dorothy Millar, worked for many years in the Church of South India. He is author of *Iona: A Pilgrim Guide*, *An Iona Prayer Book*, *Waymarks: Signposts to discovering God's presence in the world* and *Finding Hope Again: Journeying through sorrow and beyond*, also published by the Canterbury Press.

Also by the same author and published by the
Canterbury Press:

An Iona Prayer Book

A bestselling daily prayer book that follows the pattern
of worship in Iona Abbey, where pilgrims come from all
over the world.

Iona: A Pilgrim Guide

A pocket companion to this beautiful, sacred island.

**Waymarks: Signposts to discovering God's presence in
the world**

'a marvellous read for inspiration and reflection . . . all
who read it will have their spiritual awareness deepened
and their lives enriched.'

Norman Shanks, The Iona Community

**Finding Hope Again: Journeying through sorrow and
beyond**

'This is indeed "a song of hope" that has a message for
us all.' *Coracle*

www.scm-canterburypress.co.uk

The Surprise of the Sacred

Finding God in unexpected places

Peter Millar

CANTERBURY
PRESS
Norwich

© Peter Millar 2004

First published in 2004 by the
Canterbury Press Norwich
(a publishing imprint of Hymns Ancient & Modern
Limited, a registered charity)
St Mary's Works, St Mary's Plain,
Norwich, Norfolk, NR3 3BH

www.scm-canterburypress.co.uk

British Library Cataloguing in Publication data

A catalogue record for this book is available
from the British Library

ISBN 1-85311-594-0

Typeset by Rowland Phototypesetting Ltd,
Bury St Edmunds, Suffolk
Printed and bound by
Bookmarque, Croydon, Surrey

Contents

Part Five: Listening to the Silence

Part Six: Rejoicing in our Interdependence

Part Seven: Engaging with Justice

Part Eight: Searching for an Authentic Spirituality

Part Nine: Encountering God's Surprises

Part Ten: Being Open to the Moment

Part Eleven: Travelling Lightly and with Laughter

For all the
members
and friends
of the
Wellspring
Community
in Australia,
whose engaged
spirituality is an
inspiration.

By Way of Introduction . . .

Recently I was with a close friend as she celebrated her 100th birthday. Despite the frailty of her body, Margaret is still alive to the wonder and surprise of each new day. That is an amazing quality – a dimension of the soul – and being with her always reminds me of God's goodness and joy.

My visits with Margaret also bring into focus the many people, on every continent, who are living lives of deep compassion in our uncertain world. Some of them are committed Christians. Many belong to other faith traditions. Yet the majority, at least in many western countries, are not linked to institutional religion in any way.

In this book I have reflected on a few themes which I feel make sense for many of us as we seek to be both aware of what's going on in the world, and live as people with a spiritual dimension.

In recent years I myself have come to know a fair bit about personal loss and loneliness – an experience which has brought me close to many others in our world who travel on a path of heartache and uncertainty. Few of us are free of some kind of inner struggle, yet it is our very vulnerability which I believe allows us to encounter our inner depths – these places where we meet God, and our true self.

For many years my home was in India, but even before going there I had been interested in the great faith traditions of the world. I have always known that my own spiritual understanding can be enlarged and made more authentic through contact with these traditions and with those who follow their teachings. That is a conviction which lies at the heart of this book. In our interconnected world there is no place for religious intolerance. One of our essential tasks, at this particular time in human history is to reach out to 'the stranger' and listen to their story.

For many years I have had the privilege of being a member of the Iona Community which is an ecumenical and international Christian community with its roots in Scotland. The Community has taught me much about meaningful prayer, and about an engaged Christianity which takes seriously the injustices, diversity and extraordinary possibilities of our time. I think it would be fair to say that the various threads in this book reflect some of the issues with which the Iona Community is grappling as it seeks to respond to a worldwide interest in both its spirituality and commitment to local and global realities.

In a world where millions of our sisters and brothers are without even the basic necessities of life, I find it almost unbelievable that some churches spend endless amounts of time and energy debating trivial matters. Such discussions turn me off, as they do many others! On the other hand, I long to be more spiritually aware, and to have a greater understanding of God's purpose for my brief life on earth. How do we 'listen to God' in a world of busyness and noise? Perhaps the increasing interest in meditation and contemplative prayer is an indication of our longing to discover more about our soul.

On an early spring morning in 2001, my wife and soulmate Dorothy died in the arms of my son and myself, without a moment of warning. A year after her death, I wrote a book called *Finding Hope Again: Journeying through sorrow and beyond*. Many who read the book wrote to me and shared something of their own spiritual journeys. I loved these letters for they affirmed my belief that even in dark times people can discover new hope and purpose. The letters also spoke of that kind of spirituality which is able authentically to embrace both life's burdens and its beautiful moments.

All of which brings me to the small village of Laggan in the Scottish Highlands where I have a home amid the mountains and forests. I am often away from this beautiful place, but every time I return I am aware of the sacred in myself and of the sacred universe of which I am a tiny part. And it is this knowledge of the sacred which today must propel all of us to work for peace, to walk more gently on our wounded earth, and to see in the stranger's face the image of the One whose love, healing and wisdom enfold us all.

Peter Millar
Laggan, July 2004

Suggestions for Using this Book

- It is essentially a book for busy people who have not much time for reading long books, but who are searching for more depth in their life.
- The book is not intended to be read straight through from cover to cover.
- Each reflection stands on its own, although a connecting thread runs through the book.
- A reflection may provide a starting point for looking at a Bible passage or for meditation or for action – or all three!
- A small group may use this book by each member of the group reading a different page and then sharing their thoughts.
- Allow your own story, with all its pain and beauty and hope, to connect with the reflections offered here.
- One of the reflections, or several of them, may suggest ways in which you can become more aware of local and global issues.

Poems, prayers and reflections not otherwise acknowledged are by the author.

Part One

Awakening to Creation's Goodness

Go gently, my friends;
feel the good earth
beneath your feet,
celebrate the rising of the sun,
listen to the birds at dawn,
walk gently under
the silent stars,
knowing you are on holy ground,
held in love –
in the wonder of God's creation.

The Circle of the Creator

I am walking on the earth;
the earth is my mother.
Wherever I walk
I will be home.

I am walking with the people
who love me;
their love surrounds me.
Wherever I walk
I will be loved.

I am walking on the circle
of the Creator;
Creator above,
Creator below.
Wherever I walk
I am with the Creator.

I am walking upon the earth
with people who love me;
we are walking on the circle
of the Creator.

I will always be home.
I will always be loved.
I will always be
with the Creator.

Indigenous American (source unknown)

Darwin's Banyan

The suburbs of Darwin in Australia's Northern Territory are distinguished by native banyan trees. These trees get their name from a nomadic tribe in India who used them as places of shelter. The botanist George Brown who lives in Darwin has a particular love of these trees. At one time he was mayor of the city. George's words reflect his devotion to these magnificent trees:

There is a huge feeling for banyan trees in Darwin, particularly after Cyclone Tracy. They acted as debris collectors so many homes were actually saved by them. People just love them. One guy bought a house simply because it had a very large banyan in the yard. Banyans do everything that a tree is supposed to do. They give food and shade and shelter for people and animals. I mean that there are thousands of creatures living in there. Kids swarm all over the trees. Sometimes I don't understand why we bother to install playground equipment in our parks, when you have trees like this.

There is an old Aboriginal story about the trees. The way the roots hang down to the ground, the mothers used to frighten their children at night. They'd say, 'If you're not home the Banyan will get you.' There is a banyan growing out on the sand dunes across from an area of the city called Nightcliff which is said to be the site of the last spear fight between Aborigines and white people in Darwin.

Peter Solness, Tree Stories

For Everything
The great banyans give us;
Shade

Fun
Beauty
Protection
Food
Shelter
Good memories
We give thanks.

A Winter Morning . . .

It was a calm wintry morning and a light covering of snow clad the mountains surrounding our cottage. The whole land appeared to be resting under its winter blanket. The temperatures were low and the narrow road beside the house was layered with ice. The bare larches carried only minimal reminders of spring. Our local buzzard, perched high on a pine observed the frozen fields in the valley below. Everything was still, yet the scene was vibrantly alive. It was shimmering, gleaming – a great white vista enfolded in a February sun.

The clarity of light across the hills and valleys was breathtaking. I felt connected to it all – at one with the elemental purity of creation. Looking across these glorious mountains, I imagined, just for a moment, a planet devoid of chemical waste, of acid rain, of choked rivers, of wounded forests. A planet free to sing its own song, in its own time.

Carole Forman in her song 'Antarctica' also envisioned this clarity in creation . . .

> Imagine a land of long white vistas,
> Ice cold saviours,
> Gleaming glaciers,
> Breaking into the sea.

Imagine the Earth without on oil slick,
Free of pollution.
No radioactivity.

Imagine a place on Earth so awesome,
So vast so pure,
We can hardly breathe its air.
Imagine the Earth alive with morning,
Shimmering white nights,
No end of sky,
No end of sea.

Carole Forman, 'Antarctica', in Elizabeth Roberts and
Elias Amidon, eds., Earth Prayers

Dun I

Dun I simply means 'hill of Iona' and at 332 feet above sea level it is the highest point on the island. Hardly Mount Everest, but to thousands of pilgrims just as special!

Despite being a tiny hill, the view from the summit is breathtaking, in any season. To the north lie the Cuillans of Skye; to the east Ben More, the highest mountain on Mull; to the south the Paps of Jura, while lying to the west is the lighthouse of Skerryvore, several miles off the shores of Tiree. Closer to the north lie the Tresnish Isles and the island of Staffa, famous for Fingal's cave and its puffins. And looking down on Iona itself one can see a small rise close to the shore at the north end of the island, called 'Hill of the Seat' where Columba is reputed to have sat in meditation. And one can also see clearly 'The White Strand of the Monks' a beautiful beach where, on Christmas Eve in the year 986, the abbot of Iona and 15 monks were slaughtered by Viking raiders.

*   *   *

In the biblical tradition, mountains and hills have been understood as places of vision and of transfiguration. Something of that is captured in a poem by Jenni Fuchs, a Youth Associate of the Iona Community.

> Wind blowing in my face,
> Clinging to the rocks,
> At the mercy of nature's forces,
> I can't breathe – for the power of it.
>
> Sun kissing the sea goodnight,
> Distant hills bathed in shades of pink,
> Clouds gathering to great castles in the sky,
> I can't breathe – for the beauty of it.
>
> Colours fading slowly,
> Darkness descending,
> Deep peace closing in,
> I can't breathe – for the immensity of it.

Jenni Sophia Fuchs, in Neil Paynter, ed., This is the Day

Weave a Garment

> O our Mother the Earth,
> O our Father the Sky,
> your children are we,
> and with tired backs
> we bring you gifts
> that you love.
>
> Then weave for us
> a garment of brightness.

May the warp be the
white light of morning.

May the weft be
the red light of evening.

May the fringes be
the falling rain.

May the border be
the standing rainbow.

Then weave for us
a garment of brightness
that we may walk fittingly
where grass is green.

O our Mother Earth,
O our Father Sky.

Tewa Pueblo prayer

No Plant in the Ground

O Lord, our Lord,
Your greatness is seen in all the world.

Psalm 8.1

These words of the Psalmist are beautifully echoed in an old Gaelic prayer which allows our hearts to sing of the wonder of creation. I personally think that the Psalmist would have been very much at home with this Celtic vision!

O Christ, there is no plant in the ground,
but it is full of your virtue.

There is no form in the strand,
but it is full of your blessing.

There is no life in the sea,
there is no creature in the ocean,
there is nothing in the heavens,
but proclaims your goodness.

There is no bird on the wing,
there is no star in the sky,
there is nothing beneath the sun
but proclaims your goodness.

From The Iona Community Worship Book

Relatives of All that Live

'Teach us to walk as relatives of all that live.' These grace-filled words form part of a famous indigenous American prayer. Many years ago when I first read them, it came home to me forcibly just how disconnected my life was from 'every living thing'. Intellectually I may have understood that I was in some way related to all that lives upon the earth, but it was a truth which did not at that time illumine my soul. It did not go deep down. Yet as we open our minds to indigenous wisdom, we can retrace something of this lost pathway. Allowing our essential interconnectedness with all things to re-mould our ways of understanding both of God and of the created world around us.

Grandfather Great Spirit
all over the world the faces of living ones are alike.

With tenderness they have come up out of the ground.
Look upon your children that they may
face the winds and walk the good road to the Day of
    Quiet.
Grandfather Great Spirit
fill us with the Light.
Give us the strength to understand,
and the eyes to see.
Teach us to walk the soft Earth as relatives of all that live.

Sioux prayer

This notion of a richly sacralized world may still seem strange to those of us who live in a secular landscape. But can we survive without a sense of mystery and of sacredness? Spirit and matter are not two different layers of reality, two different layers of the universe. No matter where we immerse overselves in the stream of reality, we can touch the spiritual source. Either we believe that God is in all things – at the heart of matter – or we don't.

Note from Fiji

Ilaitia S. Tuwere is a Fijian scholar who teaches at a university in New Zealand, but often returns to his native shores. Recently he wrote a book, *Vanua: Towards a Fijian theology of place*, which is a refreshing insight into the links between the Fijian vanua (land) and theology. It is also about the work of reconciliation within Fiji's multiculturalism and the search for Fijian identity.

In the West we tend to understand the land in terms of what we can get from it, but Fijians, as Tuwere points out, see it very differently. As we seek to become more conscious of how to protect our own environment, we can learn much from this 'reading' of the land.

For Fijians, the land has its own laws based on a sacred organizing principle that is observed as much as it is respected. There is a 'right' time to plant vudi as well as yams, for balolo to appear on the reefs, for harvest, and for offering of the first fruits. The right time refers not only to right season, but also to religious connections with the sacred or the idea of the holy. This living memory within the human community must be given due consideration in our technological society. The sense of the holy is the presence of a unifying cosmic force that enables people to live a life attuned to peace and stability within the vanua and thus within the wider world of nature.

> May the way of the vanua be firm,
> May the custom of kinship be stable.

From a Fijian ceremonial blessing
I. S. Tuwere, Vanua: Towards a Fijian theology of place

The Blue Crane

There is a quality about the poetry of the late Judith Wright – the great Australian poet who died just six months after the twenty-first century began – which is timeless. Her lines invite us in to a sense of the sacred, of awe. Her words would speak in any age, and often draw us into the Dreaming and legend of Australia's indigenous peoples. Judith was not an Aboriginal, but in many ways she had the heart and insight of an indigenous woman.

One of her poems is about a blue crane fishing for his evening meal at twilight. She reminds us that this bird has fished there longer than our centuries, and is the true heir of both lake and evening. The crane and the landscape which he inhabits are as one. They are in harmony, and earth itself sings of this interdependence. Here we encounter not domination of the land, but an example of that unique balance among all living things which lies at the heart of Aboriginal belief.

As I reflect upon Judith's beautiful blue crane quietly searching for his supper, I think about our own inability to recognize the sacredness of the natural order. Despite endless warnings, we continue to plunder and pollute the land – forgetting that it is also the place of encounter with the living God in all of his or her mystery.

The people of Israel well understood this revealing aspect of the earth, for in the book of Exodus we read that the desert was a place of covenant where the mutual bonding of God and humankind was sealed. This lonely landscape was no neutral place, but the place of listening and of response to God's calling. In that sense God was at the heart of the landscape, embedded in it – inviting those who had eyes to see and ears to hear into an understanding of eternal truth.

It took me many years to awaken to this knowledge of sacredness, and to realize this intimate connection between the Creator, the natural order and humanity. And now that my eyes are open, so to speak, the blue crane can never be a mere object in the landscape, but is rather a powerful witness to God's glory. That fact fills me with joy. Not a momentary feeling like a warm fuzzy which is sometimes gone in an instant, but rather the joy that comes from knowing that I am a tiny part in this amazingly complex, limitless web called life. And that pulsating at the very heart of this life are the multiple, constantly unfolding energies of God.

> *God of bush and bog-myrtle,*
> *Of old man banksia and dancing birch,*
> *Of sheltering banyan and red rowan,*
> *Of whispering aspen and huon pine,*

Of heather and of eucalypt,
Illumine our minds
That we may embrace
Your sacred earth
With a renewed tenderness
Imbued with wisdom
And rooted in wonder.

Earth's Music

Great Spirit,
give us hearts to understand,
never to take
from creation's beauty
more than we can give;
never to destroy wantonly
for the furtherance of greed;
never to deny
to give our hands
for the building of earth's beauty;
never to take from her
what we cannot use.
Give us hearts to understand that
to destroy earth's music
is to create confusion;
that to wreck her appearance
is to blind us to beauty;
that to callously pollute
her fragrance
is to make a house of stench;
that as we care for her
she will care for us.

From a United Nations environmental programme

- Read these words again very slowly.

- Spend a few minutes in silence pondering just a phrase or a couple of lines.

- Think what you could do today to hear earth's music more clearly.

- Let a deep compassion for the earth fill your heart.

    The mountains, I become part of them . . .
    The herbs, the fir tree, I become part of them . . .
    The morning mists, the clouds, the gathering waters,
        I become part of them . . .
    The wilderness, the dew drops, the pollen,
        I become part of them.

Navajo chant

The Rocks Pulsate

George MacLeod, founder of the Iona Community, wrote many powerful prayers. This is one of my favourites.

        Invisible we see you,
            Christ beneath us.

        With earthly eyes
            we see beneath us
                stones and dust
                    and dross,
            fit subjects
            for the analyst's table.

But
with the eye of faith
we know you uphold.

In you
all things consist
and hold together:

the very atom is light energy,
the grass is vibrant,
the rocks pulsate.

All is in flux;
turn but a stone
and
an angel moves.

George F. MacLeod, *in* The Whole Earth Shall Cry Glory

Awaiting the Dawn

Penny and Tom are two friends in Australia who in recent
years have become involved in the work of reconciliation
between Aboriginal and white Australians. This has led
them to explore Aboriginal spirituality. They are also interested in the underlying connections between the Aboriginal
world-view and that of the Celtic church. They love walking in the Australian bush, almost as much as I do!

Dear Penny and Tom

You were asking me what attracts me to Aboriginal
spirituality and I think there are many answers, but
perhaps above all it is the knowledge, passed down
through tens of thousands of years, that all of life is sacred

and is held in a sacred balance. It is a spirituality of connection in which human beings are at one with the natural order. There is not the sense of domination of nature which marks our western relationship to the earth. At its heart the Aboriginal world-view is about harmony and also about 'listening' to the cries of the earth.

I would like you to ponder over this poem which was written by an Aboriginal woman, and sent to me by one of her friends. I think it says many important things about Aboriginal spirituality, and I hope it reaches into your depths as much as it does into mine.

This peace that fills my heart within
Rises from the earth beneath my feet
And as I await the dawn to greet
I see the leaves blowing in the wind
Across the path where my people roamed
For thousands of years since time began
Treading firmly over grass, sand and stone
Beside cool waters, across the dusty plains
To hunting grounds, corroborees and waterholes
This land was theirs, this land is mine.

I sat beside the waters cool
The shady gum trees swaying to and fro
I heard the voices through the trees
Whispering softly, clearly across the silent pool.
Ancestral songs were sung to me
Of heroic deeds of long ago,
Of dancers, singers, hunters bold,
Of our creation their stories told.
Their dreaming songs were shared with me
This land was theirs, this land is mine,
This land was theirs, this land is mine.

Nugi Gammara

It is this spiritual connection with the earth that we must find again, if we are to survive as peace-loving human beings. The encouraging thing is that many people are now becoming aware of this, and listening to the voices of nature in new ways. Aboriginal spirituality has an important task in opening up our awareness. It's a journey of healing, both of mind, spirit and body.

Let's be in touch soon.

Peter

Part Two

Welcoming the Stranger

We saw a stranger yesterday,
we put food in the eating place,
drink in the drinking place,
music in the listening place,
and, with the sacred name of
the triune God,
he blessed us and our house,
our cattle and our dear ones.

Gaelic blessing

Mike's Note

Mike is a friend in Scotland whose sister Lynda died from cancer when she was 19. A searcher after truth, and a person of compassion, he would be devastated if he could not play his weekly football match.

Dear Peter

When I met you the other day, you asked about my work as a volunteer at the local hospice for folk with cancer. I wanted to tell you more, but had to get back to the office.

Lynda, my sister, was 19 when she died in this same hospice. I hated the place at first, and did not want Lynda to go. But I've changed. I used to be a total fitness freak, then when I saw Lynda's body going away – she was a swimmer – I began to think differently. Our bodies don't seem to matter all that much; it's what's inside.

Some months after Lynda died I went back to the hospice to say 'hello' to some of the staff. I think they are magic. Before I knew what I was saying I said that I'd come as a volunteer. And I did, much to my own surprise!

At the hospice, no one forces themselves on you. You come and go – and there is always a welcome. You can be yourself. It's peaceful, and they don't preach at you. I do odd jobs. After a couple of weeks I began to get close to some of the patients. One of them thinks of me as her 'toy boy' and we joke around.

Next year I'll be 25. I've new directions, and would like to go into social work. I think more people of my age should offer as volunteers. They asked me to go and speak with a guy – same age as myself. He was so sick. It was hard, but now he looks forward to seeing me. I don't think he'll be around for long.

I miss Lynda and try to support mum and dad. I sometimes think about religion. We've never had anything to do with it, but one of the chaplains took Lynda's funeral, and it was nice. He seemed like a regular bloke. He was a friendly guy and seemed to know what we were going through. After the funeral he gave me a hug. Just gave me a hug and said nothing. Now I do that myself to some of these folk in their beds at the hospice. It's all you can do sometimes.

Cheers

Mike

PS Still playing football. I won't give that up!

Listening

Listening
is
the
highest
form
of
love.   *Paul Tillich*

The theologian Paul Tillich spoke to many people through his writing, and here he reminds us of a simple, yet powerful truth. Amid our endless words and chatter, can we also be still and possess that gift of the gentle art of listening –

both to our own inner voice and to that precious – and often hidden – voice in the other person?

To really hear what the other person is saying is a work of love, of acceptance, of wisdom. Perhaps as Tillich suggests 'the highest form of love'.

> *God of deep quiet,*
> *Still my soul,*
> *My heart,*
> *My mind,*
> *That I*
> *May listen*
> *In such a way*
> *That*
> *My listening*
> *In itself*
> *Becomes*
> *An act*
> *Of*
> *Love.*

Dr Salah's Faith

It would be possible to write a book about Runa Mackay, a member of the Iona Community, and still not have covered anything like half of her extraordinarily rich, caring and risk-taking life. Much of Runa's life has been spent working as a doctor in various parts of the Middle East, where she is valued as a confidante, friend and counsellor by countless people.

Quite apart from her extensive medical work, her skill with languages, coupled to an earthed spirituality, has enabled Runa to be an important bridge-builder between Muslim and Christian. She is a listener, and in that listening to 'the other' has built up vast reservoirs of trust in places of suspicion.

Her witness to truth is for me a beacon of light at a time when many Christians are only interested in converting Muslims. The tenderness and transparency of Runa's encounter with her friend Dr Salah belongs to the heart of God. Or to put it another way – it is something beautiful for God.

> Dr Salah suddenly asked me one day, 'Do you believe in God?' I replied, 'Yes, I could never have done what I have been able to do if I had not had a firm faith in God, and it is my faith that keeps me going even though things do look bleak.'
>
> He said that he, too, had only been able to survive throughout the years of the civil war in Lebanon and to participate in the struggles of his people because he believed in God.
>
> He is a Muslim, I am a Christian, we both have our different beliefs and ways of worshipping God, but we both believe in a God of Justice and Mercy.
>
> Runa Mackay, 'A God of Justice and Mercy', in Exile in Israel:
> A personal journey with the Palestinians

And in valuing the faith traditions of each other, Runa and Dr Salah reminded me of these words from the Qur'an:

> Hast thou not seen how all in the heavens and in the earth uttereth the praise of God? – the very birds as they spread their wings? Every creature knoweth its prayer and its praise, and God knoweth what they do.

Guru Nanak's Insight

When I read about the conflicts between the different religions in modern India, a country which was my home for several years, I think back to the vision of people like the Sikh scholar Guru Nanak.

Philosophers and saints such as Chaitanya and others of the fifteenth and sixteenth centuries belonged to an age of spiritual development in India where the concern was not only with the inner mind, but also with a person's whole being and activity. Faith and daily actions could not be separated, and we saw this truth being expressed in the way great souls like Gandhi and his colleague Vinoba Bhave led the movement for the independence of India in the last century.

The work of Guru Nanak and of the subsequent Sikh Khalsa movement was astonishingly original and renewing. It was an outburst of fresh creativity, based on an assimilation of the past, but looking to the future. Guru Nanak saw that the great religions of India must live in harmony, each tradition respecting the rituals and belief-systems of the other. He said, 'Truth is high, but higher still is truthful living.'

Our media in the West show the violence rooted in India's religious conflicts, but it is important that we also honour the communal harmony which is present in many places. In every part of India there are ordinary people giving their lives for what Guru Nanak called 'truthful living'. And like Gandhi they continue to inspire our human family.

From the seventeenth century comes this Sikh prayer written by Govind Singh:

Lord, Thou bestoweth love and Thou givest thyself to all;
Thou art the protector of life and the giver of blessing;

Thou art the cure of all sorrow and suffering,
In all shapes and everywhere, Thou art dear to me.
Thou art our vow, our beginning and our end.

Govind Singh, in Barbara Greene and Victor Gollancz, eds.,
God of a hundred names

Shut Up and Pedal

This is the title of my friend Pat Burvill's autobiography.
For 12 years, Pat worked as a nurse in a rural area of
Thailand, treating literally hundreds of women and men
who had leprosy. It was a work of love, although as Pat
says in the Introduction to her book:

There is so much more to these rural folk than the leprosy which has destroyed their extremities and defaced
their outward appearance. Leprosy is not the last word
on them; they are more than their leprosy, and they have
much to teach me of hope and trust in God.

Pat went to Thailand certain that she had the right Christian answers to life. Her work in Thailand revealed otherwise. She soon saw how limited her understanding of God
actually was, and how impoverished her knowledge of
other cultures. She writes:

I have moved from being a 'fundamentalist literalist' –
the Bible says, full-stop, everything worth knowing is
contained within its pages, no questions entered into –
to one who has no ready answers, yet a strong belief
that God is present in all people, and I have a desire to
reach out with open hands to touch, to interact with *the
other* in each person.

Pat Burvill, Shut Up and Pedal

She quotes some words which underline her belief in that openness to *the other*: 'I myself am not holy, and you may not be particularly holy, but the space between us is holy ground.'

> There is dignity here –
> we will exalt it.
> There is courage here –
> we will support it.
> There is humanity here –
> we will enjoy it.
> There is a universe in every child –
> we will share in it.
> There is a voice calling through
> the chaos of our times:
> There is a spirit moving across
> the waters of the world:
> There is movement.
> a light.
> a promise of hope.

Philip Andrews, 'The Song of the Magi' in Ron O'Grady and Lee Soo Jin, eds., Suffering and Hope

The Tune of the Other

Hanan Ashwari has been one of the significant Palestinian peace negotiators for several years. Her face is familiar to many of us around the world who follow the Palestinian/ Israeli conflict in all of its incredible complexity and sorrow.

Living in a place of constant violence has brought home to this courageous and articulate leader the need to emphasize human bonds rather then human divisions. As a woman who holds an important place in Palestinian society, she has brought particular insights to the long struggle for peace between the communities. It must seem on many days that this is an almost impossible task given the depth of suspicion and hatred.

In these lines, she speaks not as a distinguished leader of her people, but as a homemaker, of a way into peace – that peace which comes when we can awaken from our prejudices and recognize what binds us together in our human story.

> Women make things grow:
> sometimes like the crocus,
> surprised by rain, emerging fully grown
> from the belly of the earth;
> others like the palm tree with
> its promise postponed
> rising in a slow
> deliberate spiral to the sky . . .
>
> Women make things . . .
> and as we, in separate
> worlds braid
> our daughters' hair
> in the morning, you and I,
> each
> humming to herself, suddenly
> stops
> and hears the
> tune of the other.

Hanan Mikhail-Ashrawi, in Janet Morley, ed.,
Companions of God: Praying for peace in the Holy Land

Terrorism

For many years, Konrad Raiser headed up the World Council of Churches, a body which has always sought to relate Christianity to contemporary issues, both global and local. After the events of the 11 September 2001 in the United States, Konrad wrote an open letter to various Islamic communities. Part of that letter said:

> The language of threat and the logic of war breed violence. As long as the cries of those who are humiliated by unremitting injustice are ignored, terrorism will not be overcome.

Some people find it hard to connect injustice and terrorism, but as we see in many of the prophetic passages in the Old Testament, it becomes clear that unless a nation acts with justice and fairness there will not be peace among people.

In these violent times we must constantly try to understand why so many of our sisters and brothers in many areas of the world are resorting to terrorist activity. We rightly condemn terrorist attacks, but while we repudiate them, we must also listen to the cries of those who are dispossessed. This is a hard task, especially for those in positions of affluence and relative security. It demands of us all a shift in consciousness, as we continue to awaken to our global connectedness.

Pedro Casaldauga of Brazil invites us to deeper prayer, and a tougher political analysis, in these powerful words:

> Against the orders of hate
> you bring us the law of love.
> In the face of so many lies
> you are the truth out loud.

Amid so much news of death
you have the word of life.
After so many frustrated hopes
you have, Lord Jesus, the last word –
a message of truth for us all.

Pedro Casaldaliga, 'Misa dos Quilombos', tr. Tony Graham

Interconnectedness

The peace activist, writer and visionary Joanna Macy has been one of my mentors. Her extraordinary awareness of our global interconnectedness continues to awaken new depths of hope in my own heart. Joanna keeps reminding us of how we must own our sorrows, shame, anger, dread and weariness, and constantly link them to a wider reality.

We own our sorrow – and let it connect us with all who suffer the assaults on life – the victims of violence and war.

We own our shame – and let it reveal our connections with the weapons-makers and generals and politicians whose greed for profits and power led our people into this dark way.

We own our anger – and let it link us with all who are betrayed. All from whom the war-makers would divert our gaze. The hungry and homeless in our cities, and the children whose future we prepare.

We own our dread of what lies in store for us – and let it remind us of all who walk the roads of the world in fear.

We own our weariness – and let it connect us with our ancestors, who tired, too, as they struggled forward through countless ordeals, in oppression and exile and

long marches through the ages of ice. And so we connect
with their endurance, too. They did not give up.

Though hard to bear, the sorrow and shame, the anger
and fear and fatigue – each is a gift. For each can bring
into focus our deep, invisible interconnections in the
web of life. And lift us out of our narrow selves, and
bring us into community across space and time. Each
can open us to the boundless heart.

Joanna Macy, in Michael Hare Duke, ed., Praying for Peace:
Reflections on the Gulf crisis.

East 53rd Street

Who are you, my neighbour,
on this crowded street?
We live close by
in our tiny apartments
and share the changing seasons.
But do we know each other
not as strangers, but as friends?
Your family is far away, like mine:
yours in El Salvador, mine in Scotland –
two different worlds.
You came as a refugee, I through choice
and now we're on the same street
alone, in our tiny apartments
separated only by a wall.
And around us a vast city
glittering, yet vulnerable,
where so many like us
have found food and shelter
but not always freedom from fear.
Let's meet and talk one day
and share our stories,

and maybe our tears.
For the lights on our street
are Christmas lights –
reminding us of another Story
where strangers meet
and find each other.
It's the story of Jesus,
the One who is always here
on East 53rd Street
in south Chicago.

Bidwill in Sydney

Anne works as a community minister within the Uniting
Church of Australia, and is based in Bidwill, in western
Sydney. She is a former leader of the ecumenical Wellspring
Community (a community inspired by the Iona Community) and is well known for her work alongside Aboriginal communities. Anne sees the funny side of life, even in
apparently impossible situations.

Dear Anne
    Everytime I hear about your ministry in Bidwill [an
area of social need in Sydney's western suburbs] I think
of the time we all worked together there.
    You and your team have worked so hard to bring the
various cultures in Bidwill together – while at the same
time honouring the great diversity which exists in that
area.
    Even though you sometimes feel that there are miles
still to go, I think miracles have happened in these last
few years. And I don't use the word 'miracles' lightly!
    In a way, Bidwill is a microcosm of the world, with all
its various cultures and languages living side by side. In
drawing together folk from the Aboriginal communities,

the Pacific Island communities, and the diverse white communities, something very significant has happened. I believe that the way in which you have worked, honouring each community and listening intently to their stories in love, will provide an authentic model for intercultural activity in other places – not only in Australia.

Yet I also recognize how difficult such work is, for there are many social forces moving in the opposite directions. People who have never tried to move out of their own culture and actually listen to another one, have little idea what an immense task it is.

It certainly can't be done by government legislation, or by great committee structures, but only by the tough grind of walking day by day within the joys, struggles, fears, misunderstandings and laughter of the community.

You and the others are true pioneers, even prophets, although I know you never think in such terms!

With you on the journey

Peter

The Things that Unite

Some years ago when Bahai, Buddhist, Confucian, Christian, Hindu, Jain, Jew, Muslim, Shintoist, Sikh, Zoroastrian and other faith representatives came together in a common concern for a less divided world they found that they shared:

- a conviction of the fundamental unity of the human family, of the equality and dignity of all human beings;
- a sense of the sacredness of the individual and her/his conscience;

- a sense of the value of human community;
- a recognition that might is not right, that human power is not self-sufficient and absolute;
- a belief that love, compassion, unselfishness and the force of inner truthfulness and of the spirit have ultimately greater power than hate, enmity or self-interest;
- a sense of obligation to stand on the side of the poor and the oppressed as against the rich and the oppressors;
- a profound hope that good will finally prevail.

As global violence increases, can we be more attentive to these common threads which unite humankind? They are general statements, but as many commentators have pointed out, they can, without doubt, be made concrete in our local places. Without acceptance of a universal ethic we continue to fall apart – entrenched in our differences, unwilling to celebrate our diversity.

Part Three

Accepting our Vulnerability

We bring our broken loves,
friends parted, families torn;
then in your life and death we see
that love must be reborn.

We bring our broken selves,
confused and closed and tired;
then through your gift of healing grace
new purpose is inspired.

From the hymn 'We lay our broken world'
by Anna Briggs, in Songs of God's People

A Highland Morning

On this quiet track
in early summer
amid birch and larch and pine,
who could not
sense the sacred
and feel creation's heart of love?

Fourteen centuries have passed
since Iona's monks
trod these Highland hills,
at one with nature's pulse,
alive to crag and stream,
carrying Good News
about the One
whose energies of light
pulsate through strath and glen.

And as grouse scuttle in the heather,
I find again
that place of connecting –
where the soul,
returning home,
finds rest.

This track
is holy ground,
a sacred space
where, walking lightly,
wonder becomes my companion.

I look through the trees,
aware of the shy deer
who has grazed here
longer than our centuries,
certain heir of mountain and forest.

And as I meet her gaze,
something in my spirit
leaps with joy,
for I feel at one
with all that lives
on this glorious, Highland day.

Creator of mountain and forest
may we always walk on your tracks
with a tenderness, imbued with wisdom.

The Desert Waits

At once the spirit made Jesus go into the desert where
he stayed forty days, being tempted of Satan. Wild animals were there also but angels came and helped him.

Mark 1.1–12

Ruth Burgess who has been a good friend for many years,
has written an amazing number of the most vibrant
reflections on our spiritual journey in relation to human
vulnerability and fragility.

One morning when I was feeling in a desert place, a
Danish colleague placed in front of me one of Ruth's meditations and it was exactly what I needed at that moment!
Ruth reminds us that desert experiences, even if hard and
filled with inner struggle, can enrich our lives in ways we

could never imagine. The desert is a place of self-discovery, and it is often when we feel most bewildered that we can draw closer to God. This was the prayer-poem which affirmed me and gave me new perspective on a lonely morning.

> The desert waits,
> ready for those who come,
> who come obedient to the Spirit's leading;
> or who are driven,
> because they will not come any other way.
>
> The desert always waits,
> ready to let us know who we are –
> the place of self-discovery.
>
> And whilst we fear, and rightly,
> the loneliness and emptiness and harshness,
> we forget the angels,
> whom we cannot see for blindness,
> but who come when God decides
> that we need their help;
> when we are ready
> for what they can give us.

> *Ruth Burgess, in Janet Morley, ed.,* Bread of Tomorrow

Or, as David Steindl-Rast says in his book *The Listening Heart*, 'the answer was always quietly there, only our questions drowned it out'.

> *Lord, may my desert places sometimes, if not always,*
> *be places of self-discovery.*

Remembering Madrid

'Terrorists strike in Madrid' ran the headline. In a series of bombings on morning trains into the city two hundred people were instantly killed and hundreds were injured. A nation was in mourning. In shock. In disbelief. And the following day tens of thousands walked on the city streets in protest at this horror.

No words can describe the grief felt by those who had lost the ones closest to them. As the late Cardinal Basil Hume said in response to an earlier terrorist attack, 'Perhaps our only response to such a tragedy is silence linked to compassion.'

Shortly after hearing of the Madrid bombings, I re-read these words of Kathy Keay, which she wrote after her brother's death.

> I believe
> no pain is lost,
> no tear unmasked,
> no cry of anguish
> dies unheard;
> no man or bird
> crushed
> unseen
> without wounded hands
> which shaped
> the cosmos
> reshaping still
> the bits and pieces
> of who we are
> and what
> in spite of life's cruel 'accidents'
> we yet shall be.

Kathy Keay, ed., Laughter, Silence & Shouting:
An anthology of women's prayers

Nathan's Illness

Meff and Tony work in ministry and have known Nathan most of his life. They are close friends of Nathan's wife and parents. Both Meff and Tony have been a huge support to me in dark times, and their gentle spirituality is an inspiration.

Dear Meff and Tony

Many thanks for telling me of Nathan's illness. I was devastated to hear the news and have been thinking of Nathan and his family all morning.

Here he is, a young man of 23 and newly married, and suddenly one morning he awakes to discover that he has an extremely rare form of cancer pulsating through his body. Health one day, sickness the next.

And of course through your mind go all the questions. Why is Nathan ill like this? And so suddenly, without warning? Where have the cancer cells come from? Is the cancer caused by pollutants in the environment, or genetic inheritance, or stress, or, or . . . ? Everyone asks these questions.

And once you have gone through the questions you come back to the basic fact that strong, energized Nathan, is in fact very sick. It's so hard to take in.

I know there are many good friends around, but this kind of news takes some digesting! My heart reaches out to them because I know that Nathan's present situation is surrounded by so much uncertainty, despite the wonders of modern medicine and the skill of hospital staff.

And then you come to the question, how do you pray about this? My immediate response is to send up some kind of 'arrow prayer' – hoping that Nathan and those who walk with him in this strange tunnel will know

God's closeness. I believe in God's healing power, but my human words seem so utterly inadequate.

Yet without wanting to sound trite, there is a dimension in all of this which I have experience of in my own life. I don't know quite how to put it, but it's something about knowing that often within troubled places, God reveals new depths of hope and love.

Speak soon.

Peter

Nathan died a few days after I wrote this letter. His parents have wonderfully witnessed to God's tenderness and hope since his death.

Sleeping with a Mosquito

If
you
think
you
are
too
small
to
make
a
difference
try
sleeping
with
a
mosquito.

Dalai Lama

Olive

Shortly after Dorothy's death in 2001, two old friends, Olive and Bill were staying with me at my family's cottage in the Highlands. During this visit, Olive was involved in a car accident. She died on the spot. Bill was seriously injured, but, thankfully, recovered.

> Why
> did it happen
> on that golden
> summer's day
> on a Highland road
> in a place you loved so much?
>
> Just minutes before
> your life overflowed with
> goodness,
> wisdom,
> expectancy
> and love.
>
> Then
> in the twinkling of an eye,
> on a golden day
> on a Highland road,
> with the one you loved most
> by your side,
> you were gone
> from our midst –
> killed by an oncoming car
> on the wrong side of the road.

And when I saw
your still body,
I wept
and wept,
for in my own grief
you had held me
and spoken words
of gentle hope.
You had shared
my endless tears,
and understood.

And still, for others,
that Highland day was golden,
but my heart was breaking
on that narrow
moor-land road.

The Wrinkled Faces

When I was living near the centre of Sydney, it came home
to me forcibly just how much time and energy many people
spend on looking beautiful. Perfect bodies, perfect faces,
perfect clothes – along with a perfect lifestyle in a wonderful, cosmopolitan city. But on every street in downtown
Sydney there are also many women and men who carry no
marks of that kind of perfection. Their bodies and their
faces are wrinkled. They bear the marks of endurance and
of toil, and perhaps the majority of faces in our modern
world are like theirs.

And although they may not be 'beautiful' as defined by
the glossy magazines, they are often (at least in my books)
'spiritually beautiful' in ways which may be hard to describe
in a few words. They are folk who have seen life in its rawness
and splendour, and are still able to dance in the moonlight.

Kosuke Koyama knew the real value of these wrinkles when he wrote:

Watching the wrinkled faces and rough hands of the old Russian women, I saw that trouble produced endurance. They fended off despair by working through intolerable situations. In endurance life is taken seriously. Trouble is not avoided, but faced. There is no hope apart from troubles. Hope is against all the odds. Such hope, says Paul in the gospel, does not disappoint. Love produces wrinkles and rough hands. Hope points to the presence of the Holy Spirit in the world. These Russian women are 'theologically' beautiful. They make me think. They bring me to repentance. That which is symbolized by the 'wrinkled faces and rough hands' is essential for human life if it is to remain beautiful.

Kosuke Koyama, No Handle on the Cross:
An Asian meditation on the crucified mind

*Thank you, Lord, for giving us so many wrinkled
faces and rough hands in the world.*

An Unhappy Jonah

Jonah was very unhappy and became angry with God's demands. So he prayed, 'Lord, didn't I say before I left home that this is just what you would do? That's why I did my best to run away to Spain! Now, Lord, let me die. I am better off dead than alive' (Jonah 4.1–11).

Whatever else may be said about the book of Jonah, it cannot be denied that it contains much dramatic intensity. This is a prophet 'on fire' for God, yet extremely reluctant to follow his guidance. God had told him to go to Nineveh, the capital of the great empire of Assyria, but Jonah did not want to go there under any circumstances. So he argued the point with his Creator, questioning his judgements.

Jonah's frustration with God reminds me of a prayer written by Heather Garner of South Africa.

> God of Fire, God of Light,
> Are you the God who answers prayers?
> Can we talk to you?
> Are you ever listening to us?

> *Heather Garner*

Jonah debated with God, and asked all kinds of questions. We ask them too; dozens of them, and often it seems God is on another track. In our various ways we too scream at God. Can't you get me out of this mess? Where were you when my world fell apart? Are you actually listening?

God of the ages,
can you take a moment to hear my point of view
and all my peculiar questions
which I don't feel are strange at all.

Have We Forgotten?

> Have we forgotten
> the wonder of each day
> and the magic of each other,
> as we speak
> yet again
> these strange words
> about
> 'the war on terror' –
> in a world of violence?

Afraid of the stranger
but perhaps more
fearful of ourselves,
there's weeping in our souls –
in a world of violence.

In these uncertain times
we lock our hearts and doors,
and know we're still on the edge –
in a world of violence.

Yet even while imprisoned
in our freedoms,
our hearts still sing of hope –
if given half a chance.

We long to laugh again,
to dream a dream,
to dance in the sun –
in a world of love.

And One still calls
gently in the storm;
for in the midst of fears
there remains –
'Another Way'
resonant with Life,
and tested through the years.

The Hood of the Cobra

Shortly before her assassination in 1984, Indira Gandhi, then Prime Minister of India, gave a speech in Orissa. In that speech, she reminded her listeners about the attacking cobra – a relatively familiar sight in India.

Do we always have to live 'under threat' or can the peoples of the world actually fashion a different future?

> Never before
> Has the earth
> Faced so much danger and death.
> The hood of the cobra is spread.
> Humankind watches in frozen fear,
> Hoping against hope,
> That it will not strike.

> *Indira Gandhi*

> What has brought us
> to this place
> of danger
> beneath
> the cobra's
> spreading head?
>
> Are we forever in
> 'frozen fear' –
> enfolded in
> our bombs
> and mines
> and missiles –
> uncertain
> even of our neighbours
> and our friends?
>
> Or can
> we walk
> a different path,
> where our mines
> become bread,

and our minds
are transformed?

Frozen in fear
or empowered by new vision?

Must the cobra strike?

The Gift of Vulnerability

Often in church circles, people feel that they have to hide their vulnerability. Slowly this is changing as we are encouraged to share our stories – the wonderful stories inside us which make us the women and men that we are. They are God's stories – if we truly believe that we are created in the image of the Creator. Sometimes these stories are filled with pain and uncertainty, sometimes with hope and promise.

Joyce Gunn Cairns who is a Scottish artist has spent a lot of her time with folk in prison. Out of that experience, Joyce wrote a very simple but powerful reflection about vulnerability. I have always valued this wisdom which mirrors a dimension of human interconnection which I believe is at the heart of the gospel.

The people in prison whom I visit have honoured me with the gift of their vulnerability. Many of them are able to discern the true freedom that comes when one is stripped of all status, and it is thus that they can teach me something about the meaning of spiritual poverty. In coming to serve the poor, so to speak, I am discovering that I am poor.

Joyce Gunn Cairns, in Dorothy and Peter Millar, eds.,
Notes for a Pilgrim

Lord,
you who knew what it was to carry wounds;
help me to discover
that vulnerability
is not a weakness
but a gift from you.

Vulnerable Yet Strong

Greg is a scientist and musician whom I have known for many years. He was diagnosed HIV-positive some years ago and has been through many difficult times since. Now that he is feeling more confident about himself he hopes to help others who are in a similar situation. We both enjoy stupid jokes – the kind that other people look down upon as being too silly!

Dear Greg
   Your letters are always teaching me something about my own vulnerability, and I am really grateful for that gift – it's a blessing! Three years ago, when you told me that you were HIV-positive I knew that it came as a terrible shock, and it was made worse by the fact that you were just coming to a wonderful new understanding about yourself as a gay person. Previously, you had felt much rejection.

   It was hard to communicate with you then, because you felt both angry and abandoned by God. Perhaps more truthfully you felt that you had been judged by God because of your sexuality. I really felt unable to give you meaningful support, a fact which increased my own vulnerability and inadequacy.

   Then when we met a year ago, you told me that through it all you had become a much stronger person, and much more understanding of others. I know that you had been helped by meeting a deeply holy person who in a wonderfully tender way opened up dimensions of your spiritual life. At the time of that meeting, I was in a very fragile place both spiritually and emotionally and you helped me so much to reconnect with my inner self. You who had been through much struggle yourself, brought me a new inner confidence.

This morning I was reading a passage in Luke's Gospel. I found it spoke to me powerfully. It is in the twenty-first chapter. Jesus is watching wealthy people dropping their gifts into the money box in the temple. As he looks at this scene he sees a poor widow dropping in two little copper coins. As he reflects on this situation, he says: 'I tell you that this poor widow put more in than all the others. For the others offered their gifts from what they had to spare of their riches: but she, poor as she is, gave all she had to live on.'

Here was an 'outwardly' poor woman, yet when push came to shove she possessed a depth of faith that all the wealthy guys put together could never even imagine! Vulnerable as she was – at least by the world's standards – she carried an inner strength which enabled her to give sacrificially. She had known loneliness and perhaps even rejection, yet here she was that day in the temple, energized by a profound and living faith in God.

I have always known that part of my attraction to Christ's message lies in the fact that he intuitively under-stood two basic things about human beings (and many more). These were – firstly that all of us struggle with inner fears and failings, and secondly that these very elements in our nature can be the source of authentic holiness. That truth is at times almost impossible to grasp, but I know from my own experience – as you do too – that we can emerge from dark tunnels in a stronger state than when we entered them.

As you face up to living with the HIV virus, you are

actually becoming a richer and deeper human being for all of us who care for you. Your whole vision of life and of God is wider than it ever was. Your honesty and openness help us all to be more authentic people.

When the rich people were in the temple that day, they probably never even saw the woman with the copper coins. If they did, it is unlikely that they even acknowledged her presence. They were too pleased with themselves, and with their status in society, to be bothered with a poor woman without a husband. Yet while they passed by on the other side, Jesus saw her and told us about her because she was special.

Accepting our own brokenness is a gift that God gives us. It is also the starting place for life-giving, risk-taking new journeys which draw from our soul unchartered depths of goodness and laughter and love and wisdom and . . . much, much more.

The sun still shines and the music still plays . . . so take care and go gently.

Peter

Part Four

Nurturing Hope

Hope
is definitely not
the same as optimism.

It is not the conviction
that something will turn out well,
but the certainty
that something makes sense
regardless of how it turns out.

It is a dimension of the soul.

Vaclav Havel, Living in Truth

Liam and Megan

Liam and Megan live in an old house, set on a hillside, overlooking a valley in the Scottish Highlands. They have two beautiful cats and two beautiful parents, and a trampoline. They don't read my books.

At the time of writing, Liam is 9 and Megan is 6.

Dear Liam and Megan

It was great visiting you both the other day, and especially when we can read a story together and have lots of simple fun. I think it's absolutely wonderful when you both roll on the floor convulsed in laughter when I tell you one of my very, very silly jokes! I hope you always have such a great sense of humour.

I also have to tell you both – although it may sound a bit pompous – that being in touch with your vibrant spirituality (even if you haven't a clue what that word means) brings me close to God. That's special. Your incredible overflowing zest for life – for everything in life – is infectious. You take life head on, full-throttle, and LIVE it.

For you both, every moment brings its own surprises, rewards, tears, wisdom and music. I think a lot of grown-ups lost that rich love of life a while back! You wake up to a new day full of wonder.

Expectancy is your companion. It's not surprising that by bedtime you are totally exhausted. Exhausted by all the sheer, elemental joy of the day. 'Boredom' is certainly not a word in your vocabulary! Your clowning and your loving are a magical combination.

Here is a little poem about you both:

Liam and Megan,
filled with a zest for life,
a sense of wonder, and
glorious mischevious fun,
remind me
that God must be
terribly disappointed
that grown-ups
spend so much time
moaning and groaning!

Lots of hugs till we meet again

Peter

Amazing Grace

One of the very special stories of hope that I have encountered in recent years comes from the Truth and Reconciliation Commission in South Africa. It speaks to me at many
levels. Every time I read this story, it affirms my belief that
there are certain qualities of the soul that can transcend
even the worst forms of injustice and oppression. It is truly
a story for our time.

Imagine this scene from a courtroom trial in South
Africa.

A frail black woman rises slowly to her feet. She is
something over seventy years of age. Facing her from
across the room are several white security officers, one
of whom, Mr van der Broek, has just been tried and
found implicated in the murders of both the woman's
son and her husband some years before.

It was indeed Mr van der Broek, it has been established, who had come to the woman's home a number

of years back, had taken her son, shot him at point-blank range and then burned the young man's body on a fire while his police officers partied.

Several years later, van der Broek and his cohorts returned to take away her husband as well. For many months she heard nothing of his whereabouts. Then, almost two years after her husband's disappearance, van der Broek came back to fetch the woman herself. How vividly she remembers that evening, going to a place beside the river where she was shown her husband, bound and beaten, but still strong in spirit, lying on a pile of wood. The last words she heard from his lips as the officers poured gasoline over his body and set him aflame were 'Father, forgive them'.

And now the woman stands in the courtroom and listens to the confession offered by Mr van der Broek. A member of South Africa's Truth and Reconciliation Commission turns to her and asks, 'So what do you want? How should justice be done to this man who has so brutally destroyed your family?'

'I want three things,' begins the elderly woman, calmly, but confidently. 'I want first to be taken to the place where my husband's body was burned so that I can gather up the dust and give his remains a decent burial.'

She pauses, then continues. 'My husband and son were my only family. I want, secondly, therefore, for Mr van der Broek to become my son. I would like for him to come twice a month to the township and spend a day with me, so that I can pour out on him whatever love is still remaining within me.'

'And finally,' she says, 'I want a third thing. I would like Mr van der Broek to know that I offer him my forgiveness because Jesus Christ died to forgive. This was also the wish of my husband. And so, I would kindly ask someone to come to my side and lead me across the courtroom so that I can take Mr van der Broek in my arms, embrace him and let him know that he is truly forgiven.

As the court assistants come to lead the old woman across the room, Mr van der Broek, overwhelmed by what he has just heard, faints. And as he does, those in the courtroom, friends, family, neighbours – all victims of decades of oppression and injustice – begin to sing, softly, but assuredly,

> Amazing grace, how sweet the sound!
> that saved a wretch like me,
> I once was lost, but now am found,
> was blind, but now I see.

From Keep the Faith, Share the Peace, *a Mennonite peace and justice newsletter*

The Blue House

We no longer have to stand by empty-handed watching our patients die needlessly. We are providing treatment that is transforming peoples' lives.

Didakus Othiamba, head of an HIV/AIDS mission in Africa run by the world's leading independent medical relief agency, Médecins Sans Frontières (MSF)

In sub-Saharan Africa, at least 6,500 people are dying daily of AIDS-related complications. Worldwide, 40 million people are infected, but fewer than half a million have access to the life-prolonging drugs already freely available in the West. These drugs remain out of the reach of the poorest people and critics claim that it is too expensive and too complex in a Third World context to treat people effectively. Many believe that much more can be done to bring drugs to more communities.

Five-year-old Esther in Kenya was recently tested for AIDS. The result was positive. Her mother and sister are both dead and her father has abandoned her. In all of this misery, Esther was brought to Blue House, a pioneering HIV and TB clinic situated on the outskirts of the Mathare slums in Nairobi, run by MSF.

Esther was accompanied by the only person left who cares about her – her neighbour, Benta, who knows about Blue House because she is HIV-positive herself and is one of the fortunate few to have been put on anti-retroviral drugs. Benta's quality of life has improved dramatically. Esther also now has the chance of a much longer, better life.

The Blue House was one of the first places in Africa to offer free treatment for HIV/AIDS. It is a place of hope, for many people. A candle burning amid pain and death.

In Mathare valley
where so many suffer and die
there is a place
with an open door.
A simple place –
where wounded bodies
find relief and love.
A place of quiet hope
at the heart
of Africa's unimaginable pain.

Eating an Elephant

Sometimes a phrase sticks in your mind, keeps resurfacing,
and puts your life back in perspective.

This old African saying is one of the permanent fixtures in
my mind!

> The
> only
> way
> to
> eat
> an
> elephant
> is
> in
> small
> pieces.

> *Lord, why am I so often*
> *trying*
> *to eat the elephant*
> *all*
> *at once?*

Columba's Guidance

And now,
may kindly
Columba
guide you
to be

an isle
in the sea,
to be
a hill
on the shore,
to be
a star
in the night
to be
a staff
to the
weak.

Gaelic traditional

These poetic words invite us to seek the help of Saint
Columba as we try to be people of compassion in the
world. They conjure up many images.

The words bring to us the sacredness of the natural
world, and in a sense hold us in their quiet certainty.

Every time I read them, I think of Saint Columba's mission and ministry on the Isle of Iona between 563 and 597
AD. And perhaps especially that emphasis on the healing
power of Christ which was at the heart of the Celtic tradition. We too are called to be healers in our time.

- An isle in the sea — Can others see in us a place of
refuge from the storms of life?
- A hill on the shore — Can others find in us some
new inspiration, fresh affirma-
tion for their lives?
- A star in the night — Can we listen to another with
sensitivity and offer guidance?
- A staff to the weak — Can we walk in authentic
solidarity with those who feel
bruised and broken?

Anna

Anna
is
a beautiful
young teenager in our village,
alive to every possibility
that life can bring,
and some time back
on a perfectly ordinary day
when she and her pals were absorbed in
clothes and dates and exams and
what was on TV that night,
her doctor told her
that she had a rare form of cancer.

And the long, stark reality of
scans and tests,
and pills and drips
became a way of life.

Day upon day,
week upon week,
month upon month.

And then the op
and radiotherapy.

The tumour was gone
and the outlook was good –
a miracle of skill and science.

And through it all,
another miracle
threaded through our lives –

the quiet, inspiring fortitude
of an anxious family,
still reaching out to others,
enabling a whole community
to be touched in its gut
and become
'a people of love'.

George's Christmas Card

George MacLeod (Lord MacLeod of Fuinary) was the
founder of the Iona Community. George died some years
ago, but I still have with me the Christmas card which he
sent to his family and friends in 1989.

It was an unusual card to say the least, and it certainly
did not carry a traditional Christmas greeting! It was actually a plain postcard on which was printed a short message.
The words reflected a great deal about George MacLeod –
one of the truly prophetic Christian voices of the twentieth
century.

These were the words on the Christmas card:

IF YOU WISH TO GO WELL IN JANUARY
THEN:

A. EVERY SUNDAY MORNING READ ST
    MATTHEW'S GOSPEL CHAPTER 5.
B. EVERY SUNDAY EVENING READ ST
    MATTHEW'S GOSPEL CHAPTER 6.
C. EVERY MONTH TAKE COMMUNION
    AT THE NEAREST CELEBRATION OF
    COMMUNION REGARDLESS OF THE
    DENOMINATION OF THE CHURCH.
    CHRIST HAS ONLY ONE CHURCH

AND YOU ARE A MEMBER OF ITS
BODY BY REASON OF YOUR BAPTISM.
D. READ NOW COLOSSIANS 3.1–17.

Have a good Christmas

GEORGE

Seeds for the Morrow

After Dorothy's death in 2001, my daughter-in-law Ange brought together a collection of poems, prayers and wise sayings. These all came from pages in Dorothy's journal, and were pieces which had inspired her life. This collection was called *Seeds for the Morrow* which was a phrase which had encouraged Dorothy many years ago in the very early years of the international campaign to reduce the burden of debt resting on the shoulders of the world's poorest countries. Dorothy was heavily involved in this campaign from its beginnings.

Dorothy first came across the words 'seeds for the morrow' when she was reading about the life of the black preacher and activist Howard Thurman who was a mentor to Martin Luther King in the early days of the Civil Rights Movement in the States. Thurman recognized that civil rights would not come easily or quickly to his people, but fervently believed that the work they were doing to raise awareness of the injustices suffered by the black community was scattering valuable 'seeds for the morrow'. The morrow when justice would prevail.

In the last few years, Dorothy's collection has been reprinted twenty times, and has been used by individuals and groups all over the world. Although it is not in any way an expensive booklet, *Seeds for the Morrow* has also been able to raise a considerable amount of money to assist marginalized communities in areas of poverty. I have received many letters about this little book, and time and again folk have said how much they see their own work or ministry in their local situation, as scattering seeds for the future. They may not see immediate results but with Thurman, they believe that their efforts are not in vain, and that they will be blessed and bear fruit.

> *May the Spirit bless*
> *all those*
> *who in their own quiet ways,*
> *empowered by the gospel,*
> *are sowing seeds for the morrow.*

Shree Bhairav Hospital

India has more blind people than any other country and cataract is a principal cause. Throughout the country, patients often only present themselves at a hospital or clinic when their cataracts are advanced and they can no longer see.

In a remote part of Rajasthan where there has been no decent rain for five years, the Shree Bhairav Hospital is run and paid for by a Jain businessman, and all eye treatment is free and prompt.

The Jain community is strong in this rural area and within the grounds of the hospital is a beautiful temple built out of dazzling white rock. There are two salaried doctors, a Hindu and a Muslim and about fifteen local technicians working with them. There are several local nurses and, from time to time, volunteer doctors.

An average of 60 cataract operations are performed daily. There are no appointments, no waiting lists, and very sick people or those living more than 30 miles away, can be brought freely by bus from their villages thanks to the aid organization Sight Savers International. Surgical gloves and instruments are dipped in 100 per cent spirit after each procedure as it is too expensive to use disposable equipment. Incredibly there is almost no cross-infection.

Lord, thank you for this basic, hidden work of love, by people of many faiths amidst the dry and dusty villages of Rajasthan.

All Things New

Then I saw
a new heaven and a new earth,
for the first heaven and the first earth
had vanished,
and there was no longer any sea.

I saw
the holy city, new Jerusalem,
coming down out of heaven from God,
made ready like a bride adorned for her husband.

I heard
a loud voice
proclaiming from the throne:

'Now at last
God has his dwelling among people.
He will dwell among them
and they shall be his people,
and God himself will be with them.

'He will wipe every tear from their eyes;
there shall be an end to death,
and to mourning and to crying and to pain;
for the old order has passed away!'

Revelation 21.1–5 NEB (author's layout)

It's Better to Light a Candle

O God, we watch the news
and we read the headlines
about crime, cruelty and abuse.
We don't want people to be hurt –
but what can we do to help?
Light of the World, where there is darkness
Help us light a candle.

O God, we look around us
and we see that people are lonely
and unhappy. Some are unfaithful.
Some say they don't care for anyone.
We care – but what can we do?
Light of the World, where there is darkness
Help us light a candle.

O God, we live in this world.
We know there is hunger and poverty
and that so many things are unfair.
We can try to learn why;
we can raise money; we can raise our voices;
we can change the way we live.
Light of the World, where there is darkness
Help us light a candle.

O God, you came into the world
in the baby Jesus, at Christmas.
Your love is the good news
that angels told to shepherds, ordinary people.
Take us, who are just ordinary people
and help us to put our faith into action.
Light of the World, where there is darkness
Help us light a candle.

*This was written by first-year students at Tobermory High
School on the island of Mull with Jan Sutch Pickard
of the Iona Community.*

Never Burying our Dreams

Viv and Nick live in the United States and are involved in peace and justice work. They both teach in schools in the inner city. They have two young children Andrew and Hannah, and their home is a place of welcome for humans, animals and birds.

Dear Viv and Nick

Just received your photographs of Andrew and Hannah – they look fantastic, and I am sorry that I am on the other side of the world on the day of Hannah's baptism. Your beautiful kids represent our human future, and our hope for a gentler world. Just by being alive, they bring us hope! Without sounding trite, they are just a bundle of blessings for us all, and I am so happy for you both.

You asked if I could send you a prayer for sharing at the baptism and I thought of a wonderful version of the Lord's Prayer which comes from Central America. It is rooted in the daily lives of those who struggle against poverty, and because of that is about God's hope now and into the future. There are many powerful lines in this prayer, not least 'Forgive us, Lord, for keeping silent in the face of injustice and for burying our dreams'.

May Hannah and Andrew follow in your foot-steps by being on the side of the marginalized, and may they never bury their dreams.

Our Father,
who is here on earth
holy is your name
in the hungry who share their bread and their song.
Your kingdom come,
a generous land where confidence and truth reign.
Let us do your will
being a cool breeze for those who sweat.
You are giving us our daily bread
when we manage to get back our lands
or get a fairer wage.
Forgive us
for keeping silent in the face of injustice
and for burying our dreams.
Don't let us fall into the temptation
of taking up the same arms as the enemy,
but deliver us from the evil which disunites us.
And we shall have believed in humanity and in life
and we shall have known your kingdom
which is being built for ever and ever.

Thinking of you all, and may you know the gentle breezes of Christ's spirit, day by day.

Peter

Part Five

Listening to the Silence

Focus your light within us
as the rays of a beacon
show the way.

Help us breathe one holy breath,
feeling only you.

Help us let go,
clear the space inside
of busy forgetfulness.

Help us fulfill what lies within
the circle of our lives: each day
we ask no more, no less.

Neil Douglas-Klotz, Prayers of the Cosmos:
Meditations on the Aramic words of Jesus

The Void is not Silent

The void is not silent. I have always thought of it more and more as a transitional space, an in-between space. It's very much to do with time. I have always been interested as an artist in how one can somehow look again for that very first moment of creativity where everything is possible and nothing has actually happened. It's a space of becoming.

The artist Anish Kapoor is here speaking of an exhibition of his work which was held in a London gallery. The idea that the 'void is not silent' and that it is in fact a 'space of becoming' also relates to what happens in silent or contemplative meditation.

In mediation what appears as a void is actually the place of new creation. A space for new beginnings – for new movements within our inner life. And the longer we can remain in that space of stillness, of apparent emptiness, the more fruitful it becomes. This may be a paradox, but I think many have found it to be true to their own experience. It is in the void that we may hear God's gentle invitation most clearly.

May quietness descend upon my limbs,
my speech, my breath, my eyes, my ears;
may all my senses wax clear and strong
as I hear your voice
within that void
of your loving presence and peace.

Being Open to a Mystery

> In the same way the Spirit also comes to our help, weak
> as we are. For we do not know how we ought to pray;
> the Spirit himself pleads with God for us in groans that
> words cannot express.

> *Romans 8.26–28*

Carlo Carretto was an official in the Vatican when he felt
God calling him to a way of life in which he would be
alongside women and men who were exceptionally marginalized. He became a Little Brother of Jesus and lived for
long spells in the Sahara desert with nomadic tribespeople.
He wrote extensively about the spiritual life.

We can never define what prayer is
   Words are not enough for us . . .
   Yes, prayer is a mystery.
   Praying is communicating with the mystery called
God.
   Try it yourself and you will see, however skilful you
are, that you will not succeed in putting your experience
of prayer into words.
   But one aspect of it you will certainly be able to define,
when you say that it is a relationship between two
persons.
   When you pray, you will feel yourself in the presence
of Someone Else.
   Maybe you feel the Someone Else inside you.
   Maybe you feel him outside you.
   Maybe you feel enveloped in him.
   Maybe he feels far, far away from you.
   Maybe you feel him as Silence,
   as Absence,

as Aridity,
as Darkness or as Light
or as Joy or as Fulness
or as Reproof.

There are no limits to the way in which we experience
God . . .

God has always taken me by surprise, and his time
has never been mine.

Carlo Carretto, Summoned by Love

The Peace that Christ Gives

The
peace
that
Christ
gives
is
to
guide
you
in the decisions you make.

Colossians 3.15

Colossae was a town in Asia Minor, east of Ephesus, and
although the church there had not been established by Paul,
he felt responsible for it. He was also worried about some
of the Christian teaching that was going on there – in fact
he was deeply troubled by it. Among many other things,
in his letter to the Colossians he spells out the implications
of what it means to be 'in union with Christ'.

Paul points out this faith connection between the peace
that Christ brings and our personal decision-making. In
fact they are inseparable – a rather surprising truth to

modern minds. A powerful narrative in our present culture is 'personal autonomy', which seems to fly in the face of linking our decisions to God in any way. We can go it alone. I'm OK – apart from these days when I am totally stressed out!

Here is something very different. The kind of peace that God makes available to our hearts can actually inform which way we move. Can we try that one out? Perhaps especially on these days when we are hassled up to our eyeballs?

Toyohiko Kagawa in Japan, who gave his life to help folk weighed down with leprosy, once wrote this prayer: 'Unless thou lead me, Lord, the road I journey is all too hard. Through trust in thee alone can I go on.'

Dadirri

Eugene Stockton is a good friend in Australia. He is a Catholic priest and a distinguished archaeologist who has spent a lifetime walking with indigenous communities all over Australia, and learning from them.

One of his books is called *The Aboriginal Gift* (Millennium, 1995) and in it he writes of the depths of indigenous spirituality and how that ancient wisdom can bring new meaning to western spirituality. One of the people he is indebted to is Miriam-Rose Ungunmerr who speaks of what is perhaps the greatest gift Aboriginals can give to their fellow Australians, and to us all. This quality is called 'Dadirri'.

It is inner deep listening and quiet still awareness. Dadirri recognizes the deep spring that is inside us. We call on it and it calls to us. It is something akin to what we know as contemplation. Mirian-Rose says that when she experiences 'Dadirri' she is made whole again. She tells us of how she can sit on a river bank or walk through the trees – just listening, in that same way in which her community have listened since the earliest days. She knows that her people could not live good, useful lives unless they listen. This way of listening has been handed down through indigenous learning for 40,000 years.

The wonder and mystery of 'Dadirri' – an Aboriginal gift for our times.

> *Mother and Father God,*
> *Creator of the deep quiet,*
> *may we never be a stranger*
> *to that place within our heart*
> *where we are at one*
> *with life's source*
> *and tiniest bloom.*

Finding the Balance

The love of God with all thy heart and thy strength,
The love of thy neighbour as thyself.
Abide in the Testaments of God throughout all times.
Thy measure of prayer shall be until thy tears come;
Or thy measure of work of labour till thy tears come.

From the Rule of St Columba

Ian Bradley has written widely both on Columba himself and on the Celtic church. Like many others, I enjoy his books – perhaps because they are written in a clear style and carry his wide scholarship lightly.

In 1997, when I was working at Iona Abbey we remembered the fourteen hundredth anniversary of Columba's death. Around that time, Ian was commissioned by the Iona Community to write a book about the saint whom he regards as both a pilgrim and a penitent. In that book, he reminds us of the underlying basic rhythm of Christian witness held by the early Irish monks – the need to balance activity in the world and withdrawl from it. Columba's own life exemplified that rhythm from which we can learn many things. This is the picture which Ian paints of that essential balance between prayer and action, meditation and engagement.

> At times Columba was busily engaged in founding monasteries, negotiating with kings, attending councils, going on missionary journeys and ruling his ever-expanding monastic familia. Yet his biographers also portray him spending long periods praying or copying the Scriptures in his cell, and he frequently made solitary retreats.
>
> In many ways this combination of action and meditation provided a perfect example of what modern theologians call 'praxis' – a combination of involvement in practical issues and theological reflection on them. In the words of a poem written about him after his death, 'What he conceived keeping vigil, by action he ascertained.'
>
> *Ian Bradley,* Columba: Pilgrim and penitent

There is a worldwide interest, as I know from my own travels in recent years, in a Christianity which actually lives out this balance. The Iona Community, and many other Christian communities, are helping a huge number of people of all ages and backgrounds to work out ways of holding to this balance, not in special holy places but within daily living. As I think of this creative work, I give thanks for Columba's remarkable and prophetic vision lived out, with his inspirational monks, on a tiny Scottish island all these centuries ago.

Behold Iona!
A blessing on each eye that seeth it!
He who does good for others
here, will find his own redoubled
many-fold!

St Columba

Weaving a Silence

I weave a silence on my lips,
I weave a silence into my mind,
I weave a silence into my heart.

I close my ears to distractions,
I close my eyes to attentions,
I close my heart to temptations.

Calm me, O Lord,
as you stilled the storm.

Still me, O Lord, keep me from harm.

Let all
tumult
within me
cease.

Enfold me, Lord,
in your
peace.

Gaelic traditional

Blessed Insecurity

James Findlay, in his book *Merton's Palace of Nowhere* (Ave Maria Press, 2003), draws together various pieces of writing by the well-known American monk and activist Thomas Merton. As a person who often faced up to his own and the world's insecurities, Merton once wrote, 'God's enduring presence places the false self in a blessed insecurity.'

'Blessed insecurity' is not something we need run away from, but rather encounter with some degree of excitement. Perhaps even with longing. Seldom do we know our true selves, and we often present a false self to others, even to our nearest and dearest. However, Merton reminds us that God's presence – that 'enduring presence' – positions our false self quite differently. In his understanding, our false self is placed not in some no-go area but within a 'blessed insecurity'.

For most of us, some form of insecurity is a constant companion, but how often do we actually believe that it is blessed? Enfolded in the limitless compassion of our Creator and Sustainer? It's an insight worth holding to in dark days.

> You who walk,
> with us
> every step of the way,
> may we know
> that even our insecurities
> are held in the palm of your hand.

Waiting

Be patient, and wait for the Lord to act.

Psalm 37.7

Wait upon God,
with loving and pure attentiveness,
working no violence on yourself
lest you disturb the soul's peace and tranquillity.
God will feed your soul with heavenly food since you
put no obstacle in his way.

The soul in this state must remember that if it is not
    conscious
of making progress, it is making much more than it
    was
walking on foot, because God himself is bearing it
in his arms.

Although outwardly it is doing nothing,
it is in reality doing more than if it was working
since God is doing the work within it.

Let the soul
then leave itself in the hands of God
and have confidence in him.

Let it not trust itself to the hands and works of others,
for if it stays in God's care
it will certainly
make progress.

John of the Cross (1542–91)

Simple Awareness

In my journal, I have kept these words of the writer Paula Fairlie in which she describes that 'simple awareness' of knowing that God is present, even momentarily. I have found this term helpful in my own spiritual journeying. It may be that at some points in our life we become acutely aware of God's presence, and can hold on to that knowledge when our spiritual life is at a low ebb.

I was very happy. Towards evening we sat down on a small hill. Cattle were moving slowly in the deep valley and birds were swooping low beneath us. We now sat in silence, the sun still pleasantly warm on our backs. I became powerfully aware of God's presence. It was absolutely overwhelming. I had to close my eyes and could hardly breathe; his presence was almost tangible, enfolding me in the warm evening air.

This experience has never been repeated, but the happiness of it comes back whenever I feel the sun warm on my back. I understand the value of memory and appreciate the psalms in which the Israelites recalled God's saving help.

The remembrance gives one confidence in the present moment and allows one to hope in the future. Simple awareness has sometimes come to me when I have heard people talking about God or something beautiful. I would feel my heart glowing within me for the moment, in affirmation, of the recognised truth. Perhaps this is how the disciples on the road to Emmaus responded to the sensed but unrecognised presence of the Lord.

Paula Fairlie in Maria Boulding, ed.,
A Touch of God: Eight monastic journeys

Amidst the washing up
And shopping
And filling in forms
And paying bills
And worrying about the next bill
And doing the ironing
And speaking on the phone
And waiting on the bus
And feeding the dog
And paying more bills,
May there be
These moments
Of simple awareness
In which
I know I am held,
In the wonder of that Love
Where my heart
Is truly at home
And at peace.

Meeting One's True Self

Try to enter the treasure chamber that is within you and then you discover the treasure chamber of heaven. They are one and the same. If you succeed in entering one you will see both.

St Isaac of Syria (6th century)

I ask God from the wealth of his glory to give you power through his Spirit to be strong in your inner selves.

Ephesians 3.16

Coming to terms with one's inner self is a lifelong process and from my own experience, there are many sidetracks along the way! In my pastoral work I have met many people who feel spiritually discouraged because they never seem to move forward in self-knowledge. They find it almost impossible to believe St John of the Cross when he wrote, 'The soul of one who loves God always swims in joy, always keeps holiday and is always in the mind for singing.'

Yet is it not also true sometimes at that very point when all seems lost and we feel utterly abandoned both by God and other people, that a new spiritual awakening occurs? In his work, *Siddhartha*, Hermann Hesse speaks powerfully about this possibility.

> At that moment
> When the world melted away,
> When he stood alone
> Like a star
> In the heavens,
> He was overwhelmed
> By a feeling of icy despair,
> But he was
> More firmly himself
> Than ever.
>
> That was the last shudder
> Of his awakening –
> The last pains of birth.

Herman Hesse, Siddhartha, *tr. Hilda Rosner*

Many of the great spiritual guides tell us that it is only possible to enter the real depths of our spiritual self through such an awakening. The writer of the letter to the small church in Ephesus speaks of God's presence being strong in these depths, but there is no suggestion that this knowledge is to come either easily or quickly. Entering the treasure chamber that is within us all takes a lifetime, and may involve many awakenings. Yet paradoxical as it may seem, it is often when we feel most discouraged that the Spirit surprises us and leads us to deeper knowledge of our true self – that self which is the dwelling-place of God.

Transparency

Happy are those who know they are spiritually poor;
the Kingdom of heaven belongs to them.
Happy are those who are humble;
they will receive what God has promised.
Happy are the pure in heart;
they will see God.

Matthew 5.3–10

Many of my Hindu friends have told me how much they love the Beatitudes, because they offer a beautiful invitation onto the path of God. Whatever our faith tradition may be, the words that Jesus gave to the crowds on that Palestinian hillside over two thousand years ago will touch hearts for as long as humanity exists on this earth.

The Sermon on the Mount is longer than the words quoted here, but as we take up Christ's invitation concerning our spiritual poverty, our humility and our purity, I believe that we are powerfully challenged about the quality and depth of our inner transparency. And this transparency of the soul is always linked to our passion for justice, for reconciliation, for accountability, for healing and for faithful and costly engagement with the hurts of our world.

There is a rabbinic tradition that when the Messiah comes he will sit at the city gates as a beggar, and most people will just see an ugly man: 'He had no form or comeliness that we should look at him, and no beauty that we should desire him' (Isaiah 53.2). But those who have eyes to see will glimpse the radiant transparency and beauty of the Redeemer.

The transparent soul. The heart that has been open to God's purpose and possibility and set free for love. Spiritual poverty, humility and purity of heart (all counter-cultural qualities at the present time) are the foundations for a long-term faithfulness to the call of Christ. As dimensions of the soul they take us home to God's transparency. And to the reshaping of our imagination which for me means that we can look out on our bewildered world not with harshness, judgement or prejudice, but with tenderness, aware of our own wounds and contradiction.

In the stillness of our hearts, as we invite Jesus to teach us about spiritual poverty, humility and purity, we are not seeking some kind of false freedom from contamination by this world! Quite the opposite. It is more about being fully present in what we do and are, having a face and a body that expresses ourselves, beyond duplicity and deceit. It is about sharing in the vulnerability of Christ – walking in his freedom and spontaneity.

Growing in Love

I may have all the faith needed to move mountains – but if I have no love I am nothing. I may give away everything I have – but if I have no love, this does me no good. Love is patient and kind; it is not jealous or conceited or proud; love is not ill-mannered or selfish or irritable; love does not keep a record of wrongs; love is not happy with evil, but is happy with the truth. Love never gives up; and its faith, hope and patience never fail.

1 Corinthians 13.1–7

These are such familiar words to many people that they can be read quickly, but the question remains – are our souls growing in love? As the years go by are we becoming more deeply compassionate human beings? Are we moulding our hearts with violence, triviality and immediate gratification, or are we nourishing some of the qualities which Paul wrote about in his letter to the church in Corinth?

In my own spiritual journey I find these immensely difficult questions. I value the vision which Paul holds before us – I would call it an invitation to inner freedom – yet to actually live it out is another question. It is so easy to become jealous or ill-mannered or selfish or proud, and it's sometimes even easier to keep 'a record of wrongs'! I often feel that I am far away from the road of love.

A close friend and his wife have ministered in a large area of public housing for more than thirty years. If you go and talk with local people in that area they will tell you immediately that their pastor and his wife care for them – really love them. And although they would not use the term, this love has been unconditional – given freely and joyfully. That is its strength. And the local folk have responded in love – unconditionally. That is their strength.

And as I think about these particular friends and their ministry of love, it brings home to me the simple fact that Paul's vision cannot become a reality without 'the other' – or perhaps more accurately 'the others' – being present in our lives. The writer Henri Nouwen often used the words 'reaching out' in his books: reaching out to our immediate family, to the local community, to the wider world. And what made that 'reaching out' real was that it was earthed in love. Aware of God's love, we then can reach out in love.

Yet another question remains. Am I really prepared to allow God to fill my life with this unconditional love? Or would I rather hold back? As one person put it, God asked for my life and I gave 50 pence!

To live even a small part of Paul's vision is possible, for we see people all around us witnessing to it. And even on those days when I feel a long way from that vision, I realize that seeds of love are still in my soul. Of one thing I am certain – my spiritual life will never deepen unless I grow in love. And without God's help that's impossible. As the little prayer from Nepal says: 'How glad we are to know and feel the touch of Jesus' love.'

Part Six

Rejoicing in our Interdependence

Be still within yourself and know that the trail is beautiful. May the winds be gentle upon your face, and your direction be straight and true as the flight of an eagle. Walk in harmony with God and all people.

Navajo blessing

Jean's Prayer

Jean Mortimer is a minister of the United Reformed Church working in Leeds. A few years ago, Jean's younger son was diagnosed HIV-positive. In this meditation she calls on Mary who stood with her own son in his suffering to be with all those who have HIV/AIDS within their families.

Mary, Mother of God,
stand beside all mothers who watch the suffering
of innocent children in every place of crucifixion today;

in places of poverty, anguish and despair,
where medication is rationed or denied,
because someone else holds the purse-strings,
and dictates spending priorities;

in places of fragile hope and committed action,
where grandmothers, aunties and surrogate mothers
combine their efforts to bring light and love
to children, orphaned by AIDS, or infected from
    birth;

in places of fragile hope and self-giving love,
where older brothers and sisters become carers too
    soon,
parenting and providing for their families
when fathers and mothers have died.

Mary, Mother of God,
give strength to all who feel powerless
in the face of such pain;

lift up their hearts to sing 'Magnificat';
to cry 'Freedom' for all those whose lives have been
    brought low;
to raise the voice of prophesy and protest
in the corridors of power;
to proclaim the love and justice of God
for all who are marginalized or oppressed.

Mary, Mother of God,
may they rest in your compassion
and take your courage in their hands.

Jean Mortimer

Can 'Community' Return?

During the last few generations in western communities at least, the individual has become more isolated. Perhaps lonelier. Friends in Africa and India are amazed when they learn that, in our country, folk can die in their own homes and not be found for several days, even weeks. Dead behind their front door but without anyone knowing.

They find it impossible to believe that not one single other person would call at their house over the course of a few weeks. And they contrast that kind of isolation with the endless comings and goings in their own homes. It is still true that in many parts of the world it takes a whole village to raise a child.

Having said this, I also believe that our western societies are now searching at a whole variety of levels, for the restoration of 'community' – a word heard these days from even government officials. A buzz word; a warm word; part of the jargon.

So we hear of community policing, community care, community studies, youth and community work, community churches, community centres. One study listed 94 uses of the term, the only feature they had in common being a concern about people.

Despite this wide usage, the basic question remains: can 'community' in the sense of people being mutually accountable to one another ever return in a society which prizes so highly the individual and personal self-enhancement? That is a huge question, but here are words of wisdom from a Native American tribal chief.

From our approach to life there comes a great freedom – an intense and absorbing love for nature; a respect for life; enriching faith in a Supreme Power; and principles of truth, honesty, generosity, equity and brotherhood as a guide to daily relationships.

Quoted in Edward S. Curtis, Native American Wisdom

Child of the Dreamtime

I am a child
Of the Dreamtime people,
Part of this land like the gnarled gum tree.

I am the river softly singing,
Chanting our Songs
On the way to the sea.
My spirit is the dust devils,
Mirages that dance on the plains.

I am the snow,
The wind,
The falling rain,
I'm part of the rocks and the red desert earth,
Red as the blood that flows in my veins.

I am the eagle,
The crow,
And the snakes that glides
Through the rain forests
That cling to the mountainside.

I awakened here when the earth was new,
There was emu, wombat and kangaroo,
No other man of a different hue!

I am this land
And this land is me
I am Australia.

Hyllis Maris, Aboriginal writer, quoted in Dorothy Millar,
Words of Meaning

Count to Twelve

And now we will count to twelve
and we shall all keep still . . .

For once on the face of the earth
let's not speak in any language;
let's stop for one second,
and not move our arms so much.

It would be an exotic moment
without rush, without engines,
we would all be together
in a sudden strangeness.

Those who prepare wars,
wars with gas, wars with fire,
victory with no survivors,

would put on clean clothes
and walk about with their brothers
in the shade doing nothing.

What I want should not be confused
with total inactivity.
(Life is what it is about,
I want no truck with death.)

If we were not so single-minded
about keeping our lives moving,
and for once could do nothing
perhaps a huge silence
might interrupt this sadness
of never understanding ourselves
and of threatening ourselves with death.

Perhaps the earth can teach us
as when everything seems dead
and later proves to be alive.

Now I'll count up to twelve,
and you keep quiet and I will go.

Pablo Neruda, 'Keeping Quiet'

Bonhoeffer's Words

The German theologian Dietrich Bonhoeffer was executed
by the Nazis in 1943 for being involved in a plot to assas-
sinate Hitler. In his letters and papers from prison, while
awaiting execution, he spoke prophetically of what it
meant to be a follower of Christ in the midst of political
and social evil.

*   *   *

The kind of 'mistrust' to which Bonhoeffer refers here permeates many of our global situations today. Yet it was in a time infected with mistrust that Bonhoeffer discovered genuine trust.

The air in which we live
   is so infected with mistrust
that it is almost bringing us to ruin.
   But wherever we broke through
the layer of mistrust,
   we found the experience
of a trust that we had previously
   never even dreamed of.
We have learned to put our lives
   into the hands of those we trust.
Against all the ambiguity
   in which our acts and lives have had to stand
we have learned to trust unreservedly.
   We know now that we can really live
and work only in such confidence,
   which always remains a risk,
but a risk that is gladly assumed.
   Trust will always remain for us
one of the greatest, rarest and happiest gifts
   of human life in community,
and it can only arise against the dark background
   of a necessary mistrust.

Dietrich Bonhoeffer, Letters and Papers from Prison
(author's layout)

The Human Family

Imagine
shrinking the earth's population
to
a village of 100 people
with all the existing human ratios remaining the same.

The village would have –
57 Asians
21 Europeans
14 North and South Americans
and 8 Africans.

There would be 51 females and 49 males.
There would be 70 non-whites and 30 whites.
There would be 70 non-Christians and 30 Christians.
50 per cent of the village's wealth would be in the hands
of 6 people – all North American citizens.
80 villagers would live in sub-standard housing.
70 would be unable to read.
50 would suffer from malnutrition.
1 would have a college education.

These statistics have been used by many of the aid agencies

Good News and Bad News

This short item was in *The Tablet*, the well-known international Catholic weekly.

Scotland's first female rabbi, Nancy Morris, delivers
some good news and some bad news in an interview for
the Church of Scotland's monthly *Life and Work* magazine.

The good news is that Morris, a 42-year-old former lawyer from Canada, says that she has not come across anti-Semitism in Scotland. The bad news is that she thinks it is because the population is fully occupied perpetuating the Catholic–Protestant divide.

'They have been too bothered concentrating on each other to be anti-Semitic, so Jews have always felt part of the gang here,' she says.

The Tablet, 19 June 2004

When Will the Rains Come?

One day, returning to Chennai (Madras) in South India from some drought-stricken villages, these thoughts came to me.

> God, I am so comfortable,
> the water is running out of our tap
> and so near us,
> just a short bus journey away,
> there are thousands of families
> who don't even have a single drop.
>
> When will the rains come?
>
> You don't see us as rich and poor,
> but as a single family –
> connected,
> involved,
> bearing one another's burdens,
> reaching out
> in good times
> and in bad ones.
>
> When will the rains come?

But we're not equal;
we have water
they don't.
And things won't change,
not
in a day, or a month, or a year.
We'll still have water,
and the village wells will be dry.

When will the rains come?

I don't know,
nor do the villagers;
but perhaps by caring more,
my sisters and brothers
will find new strength,
even when the wells are empty.

Balm for Sorrow

It is a privilege to be invited to the funeral of an Aboriginal person in Australia. This litany was shared at one of these funerals. We were saying farewell to a young man.

The Elders gather
and we grieve with our people, Lord.

Be our comfort, Lord.

The families travel,
distance unheeded,
for comfort, assurance and presence.

Be with our Mob*, Lord

Stories are told,
love lost expressed
in tearful litanies of sorrow.

Grant us a big heart, Lord.

The young they die,
broken in body and spirit,

Give us renewal, Lord.

Song lines to sing,
proud in the old ways,
confident in the new.

Be our comfort, Lord.

May the rock of our Dreaming,†
flow springs of healing,
balm for our sorrow,
joy for tomorrow.

Kebabs and Warm Naan Bread

A group of us working at Iona Abbey prepared a prayer
of gratitude for the rich diversity of our multicultural
society. It was received with enthusiasm! This is part of it.

Lord of every nation, we thank you for:

Boogie Woogie
Be Bop
Jazz
Rap

---

* 'Mob' is an Aboriginal term for describing the family and community.
† 'Dreaming' is always spelt with a capital 'D'.

Funk
Soul
Rock'n'Roll

Salsa clubs
The samba
Spirituals
And voices
Deep as wells of living water

For the heady smell of Indian grocer-shops
For cardamom, saffron, cloves
Jasmine, patchouli, sandalwood

For the music of accents
Dance of gestures
Communication of smiles
And for the lined landscapes of beautiful faces

For kebabs
Hummus
Baklava
Goulash
Wonton soup
Warm naan bread
Tandoori
Sweet and sour
Rice and peas and curried goat

For Greek delicatessens
Arabic delicatessens
Italian delicatessens
For delicatessens!

Part of a longer prayer published in This is the Day

Kindness

Mother Teresa shared these thoughts with her co-workers in Calcutta.

> Be kind and merciful.
>
> Let no one ever come to you without
> coming away better and happier.
>
> Be the living expression of God's
> kindness.
>
> Kindness in
> your face:
> your eyes:
> your smile.
>
> Kindness in
> your warm
> greeting.
>
> In every place
> of need
> we are
> the light
> of
> God's
> kindness.

To children,
to the poor,
to all who suffer and are lonely,
give a smile.

Give them not only your care,
but your heart.

Mother Teresa

Part Seven

Engaging with Justice

If we are to take the incarnation seriously we must be concerned about where people live, how they live, whether they have justice, whether they are uprooted and dumped as rubbish in resettlement camps, whether they are detained without trial, whether they receive an inferior education, whether they have a say in the decisions that affect their lives most deeply . . .

Archbishop Desmond Tutu, The Rainbow People of God: South Africa's victory over apartheid

Gandhi's Truth

To recognize evil
and not to oppose it
is to surrender your humanity.

To recognize evil
and to oppose it
with the weapons of the evil-doer
is to enter into your humanity.

To recognize evil and to oppose it
with the weapons of God
is to enter into your divinity.

Amazing words, and prophetic in our times. But what are 'the weapons of God' – these qualities of the soul which Gandhi believed can transform even the darkest night?

Centuries before Gandhi, an itinerant preacher called Paul spoke about some of these 'weapons' to a small group in Galatia who were trying to follow Jesus. It was a mind-blowing list and still is! He told them that the Spirit as it worked in their lives brought –

LOVE
JOY
PEACE
PATIENCE
KINDNESS
GOODNESS
FAITHFULNESS

HUMILITY
AND SELF-CONTROL

Galatians 5.22–26

Letter to Mordechai

> I believed I was going to serve the human people, the
> Israelis and Arabs, because nuclear weapons kill
> everyone.

Mordechai Vanunu

Mordechai Vanunu is usually described as Israel's nuclear
whistleblower. He was born in 1954 into a Jewish family
in Morocco and ten years later moved with them to Israel.
He worked as a technician at Israel's Dimona nuclear
facility and in the late 1980s revealed to a British news-
paper some illegal photographs he had taken at that facility. These photographs proved that Israel had nuclear
bombs.

Around that time, Mordechai became a Christian. After
being captured by Israeli agents in Rome, he was imprisoned for 17 years, 11 of which were spent in solitary
confinement. He was released in the spring of 2004, and
shortly after his release a friend and I had the opportunity
to spend some time with him in St George's Cathedral in
Jerusalem where he was basically under house arrest. In
time, Mordechai hopes to settle in Europe or in the States,
for he remains a distrusted person in Israel. His life continues to be in danger.

Dear Mordechai
    It was so good to be able to have these long talks
together when I was in Jerusalem. I cannot believe that
you are so well, both in mind and in spirit after all

that you have been through during the long, hard years of your imprisonment. It was particularly good to share the eucharist with you (that was a special moment) and also to be able to share a bottle of white wine!

I know that your personal future is still very uncertain, but I wanted to tell you how much I learned from you about the Christian faith in times of persecution. What you have endured in prison, perhaps especially during the eleven years of your solitary confinement, is beyond my understanding. Although you were so welcoming and gracious when we met, I was fully aware that you carry the pain of your imprisonment. Most human beings would not have survived what you have gone through, and even now, having served your time in prison, you continue to be the recipient of much hatred and abuse. And almost daily death threats.

With millions of others around the world, we long to see our planet free from nuclear weapons. Thousands of us regard you as a hero, although what you did was seen as illegal by your government. Nuclear weapons in themselves are illegal if we are to accept the ruling of an international court. I myself am working, along with many others, for the day when my own country will be free of such weapons of mass destruction. As you say, 'nuclear weapons kill everyone'.

Perhaps what struck me most in our conversations was the way in which you have come through these unspeakable experiences with your faith, laughter, intelligence, awareness, prayer and body still intact. You are a witness to the endurance of the human spirit. I asked you when we were together what had kept you going and you said that your faith in Christ has been a significant factor. I hope that when you are able to travel, you will share your knowledge of God with many people,

for such a witness as yours is needed in our violent time.
You are an inspiration.

With warm wishes – thinking of you.

Peter

Words from Mozambique

The
success
of
the
revolution
depends
on
the
tiny
daily
acts
of
each
one
of
us.

These are words of the late President Samora of Mozambique, a country which is no stranger to all the multiple
contemporary forms of marginalization.

Most of us are far from the realities of Mozambique, yet
these words resonate in many situations, including our
own.

Many of us accept that our whole way of thinking in the
affluent nations requires radical alteration if we are to live
in a more harmonious global order. And those prophetic,

often uncomfortable voices in our midst, who are working for global structural change, are well aware that it is the 'tiny daily acts of each one of us' which will ultimately bring about change. Not the headline-grabbing statements, but that quiet faithfulness which believes that how we personally act now determines our human future.

Our 'tiny acts' may have enormous significance in the purposes of God. It was the economist, Fritz Schumacher – famous for his phrase 'small is beautiful' – who ardently believed that an ounce of practice is worth a ton of theory. Ordinary, almost unnoticeable acts, can have unimaginable repercussions. Or in Rabbi Rami Shapiro's words:

It is up to us to see that the world still stands.

Tangents: Selected poems 1978–1988

My Hands are Ready Now

The Iona Community's Wild Goose Resource Group has done a huge amount for the renewal of church music in Britain and in many other countries.

In the worship in Iona Abbey lots of their hymns are sung and cherished by literally thousands of people each year. When I worked there we often sang 'My hands are ready now', written by Jorge Maldonado, with music arranged by the Wild Goose Resource Group. It's a song of empowerment for all of us, but perhaps especially for those working for peace and justice in these often desperately hard places at the coalface.

Sent by the Lord am I;
my hands are ready now
to make the earth a place
in which the kingdom comes.

Sent by the Lord am I;
my hands are ready now
to make the earth a place
in which the kingdom comes.

The angels cannot change
a world of hurt and pain
into a world of love,
of justice and of peace.
The task is mine to do,
to set it really free.
Oh, help me to obey;
help me to do your will.

Jorge Maldonado, '*Sent by the Lord am I*',
(from Sent by the Lord: World church songs, *vol.* 2)

Servant Christ,
help us to follow you on the road to Jerusalem,
to set our faces firmly against friendly suggestions
for a safe, expedient life:
to embrace boldly the way of self-offering,
in order to make the earth a place
in which your Kingdom comes.

The Universal Prayer for Peace

This prayer has been used by millions of people of all faiths
around the world. It is based on a traditional prayer from
India, and invites us to be part of a global pilgrimage in
understanding.

On many occasions I have discovered new depths in
my own soul when saying this prayer with people whose
culture, language and religion are different, but who share

my longing for a world in which hope, trust, justice, truth, love and peace are much more in evidence in our common life.

> Lead us from death to life,
> from falsehood to truth.
> Lead us from despair to hope,
> from fear to trust.
> Lead us from hate to love,
> from war to peace.
> Let peace fill
> our hearts,
> our world,
> our universe.
> Let us dream together,
> pray together,
> work together,
> to build one world
> of peace and justice
> for all.

Homelessness

Speaking at the launch of an organization called 'Housing Justice', Rowan Williams placed the reality of homelessness in a wider context – that of broken relationships. He reminds us that homelessness compromises our own humanity not just that of the homeless person.

When we talk about homes and homelessness we're not talking simply about the physical backdrop but about how people make or are not allowed to make a physical environment of their own. A person who is homeless is a person who is in some important degree deprived of having that background that makes them in other people's eyes fully human.

They've not had the full freedom to make part of the world theirs, to put the print of their humanity upon it. And that's a reminder, of course, that the homeless person is not simply a person without a roof over their head. The homeless person is someone who is deprived in the area of relationship. Something has gone badly wrong in relationships – stripping them of the human background of love and friendship, and that execrably leads to all those tangles and problems that occur when there is no physical background, no literal home for them to make their own, no space that is theirs.

If the churches are concerned about homelessness, it is I hope and trust not just because we would like to see people, as it were, tidily housed and taken care of. It's because we sense someone living with deep breakages in their relationship is someone whose deprivation and suffering is something that eats away at and compromises our own humanity as well.

From a Sermon given by the Archbishop of Canterbury at St Martins-in-the-Fields, London, 27 November 2003

Loading our Trolleys

Like most of us, Irene Sayer is a regular shopper in supermarkets. And like many of us she is concerned at the whole imbalance in international trade and the injustices which flow from it. Irene's meditation underlines just how much we are caught up in this global imbalance.

Creator God,
we confess our carelessness
as we load our trolleys
at the supermarket.
Imported vegetables for us
can mean
diverted rivers
for others.
Our need for
out of season fruits
deprives others of water.
On the land
farmers plough in the crop
because it is not worthwhile
harvesting it.
Coffee growers in South America
grub up coffee bushes
and plant coco leaves
which end up as
cocaine on our streets.
We profess Jesus
who values people;
yet products
are more important to us
than producers.
Cheap food –
at the expense of others.
Lord,
may be become more aware of our
thoughtless self-interest and easy indifference.

Irene Sayer, in Cradle of Life,
Methodist Prayer Handbook 2003–2004

Non-Violent Peaceforce

The Non-Violent Peaceforce is an international organization dedicated to creating a large-scale peace army of
trained, paid civilians from every continent to intervene in
conflict situations.

Using proven non-violent intervention techniques,
Peaceforce teams help local peacemakers carry out and
expand their work to transform conflicts.

The Peaceforce is currently conducting a three-year pilot
project in Sri Lanka, and working with local groups in
Burma, Israel/Palestine and the Korean Peninsula.

When Mel and Georgia Duncan were working as volunteers at Iona Abbey in 1997 they spoke to me about their
vision to bring into being an international, trained
peaceforce to work in areas of conflict around the world.

It seemed like a huge vision, but now it is a reality.
Against countless odds, Peaceforce is now able to send
women and men to different countries. Even within its
short lifetime, its work has been valued in many quarters.

Mel and Georgia have taught me that a personal vision,
within a society which often appears impersonal, is vital.
They are 'ordinary' people but they do not subscribe to the
widely held view that individuals are powerless in the face
of global structures.

We are not powerless, and as I think about the folk
involved with Peaceforce, I realize again the incredible
potential within every human being.

> If you are coming to look for a couch for a soft
>   occasion
> do not trouble to enter where the most beautiful
>   flower is found.
> This is a place disposed only for sacrifice.

Here you have to be
    the last to eat
    the last to have
    the last to sleep
    the first to die.

Reflection from El Salvador, in John Carden, ed.,
A Procession of Prayers

Ellen and Helen

Ellen Moxley and Helen Steven are both members of the Iona Community and have been involved in international peace and justice work for many years. Ellen is one of the 'Trident Three' who won a major legal case in Scotland concerning the legality of Britain's nuclear submarine base in the Holy Loch in Scotland.

Dear Ellen and Helen

Many thanks for all your kindness when I stayed with you the other day. I especially valued our discussions about your work for justice and peace over many years. You continue to be a huge source of encouragement to many of us who believe that our Christian faith propels us to be actively involved in the search for real justice among peoples and for lasting peace in this troubled world.

Your own work in this area has been recognized internationally. Long after your lives are over, people will remember with gratitude your courageous and incredibly faithful stand against nuclear weapons, and in particular against the British Trident thermonuclear submarine fleet based in the Scottish Highlands. I believe that your actions have brought the world a step closer towards freedom from the threat of nuclear war, a threat which, some would say, has increased since the events of 11 September 2001 in America.

Throughout these long years of your peace-making activities, you have been sustained by what I see as a spirituality which is earthed both in God's compassion and in the cries of our increasingly violent world. You don't only talk and write about peace, but your simple lifestyle, rooted in disciplined meditation, embodies peace. I know that your spiritual insights have deepened through your long connection with the Society of Friends (the Quakers). I love the fact that you have not become exhausted by your costly witness for peace, and that you still have time for much laughter and joyful sharing with others.

One of the most important things which you have taught me is that we are not able to sustain a long-term commitment to this often tiring and difficult work of peace-making without returning time and time again to the quiet places of our soul: these hidden springs of nourishment. In being healers in the world, as you both are, we so much need to seek for healing in ourselves. There is no good campaigning for global peace if our own hearts are full of bitterness or disillusionment!

Several times you have been imprisoned because of your efforts to draw our attention to the terrible moral evil of nuclear weapons, and yet you have always made of these times behind bars something creative. They have become a significant part of your spiritual journey, while at the same time making many others think about how God wants to use their life to make the world a gentler and safer place.

I know that you are not seeking praise about your work, but as I came back from being with you I thought how much we can each do, in our own way, to bring healing among the nations. It's easy to give up and to feel powerless. You have witnessed to an alternative way

– that of sacrificial involvement with some of the issues which confront the modern world. And that involvement has been carried with gentleness, humour and courage. Can you be surprised that I find you inspiring?

Thanks again for your warm welcome and home-baking!

Peter

Pope John Paul's Prayer

During the 25 years of his papacy, Pope John Paul II has consistently called on humanity to cease from war. His prayers have echoed in the minds of many far beyond the boundaries of his own church.

> God of our Fathers,
> great and merciful God,
> Lord of peace and life,
> Father of all.
>
> You have plans of peace, and not of affliction.
> You condemn wars
> and defeat the pride of the violent.
>
> You sent your Son Jesus
> to preach peace
> to those who are near and far away,
> to gather people of every race and nation
> into a single family.
>
> Hear the single-hearted cry of your children,
> the anguished plea of all humanity;
> no more war, an adventure without return,
> no more war, a spiral of death and violence;

a threat against all your creatures
in heaven, on the earth and in the sea.

We implore you,
speak to the hearts of those responsible
for the fate of peoples,
stop the 'logic' of revenge and retaliation;
with your spirit suggest new solutions,
generous and honourable gestures,
room for dialogue,
and patient waiting
which are more fruitful
than the hurried deadlines of war.

Give our era days of peace.
War no more.

A prayer used at one of Pope John Paul II's
interfaith peace meetings

A Hard Task

The words 'seek peace and pursue it' are familiar. As we
ponder on these words, it's clear that we have to run after
peace, put all our energies into making it possible, dedicate
our thoughts and intentions to being a 'person of peace'.
In other words, it won't come without our desire and commitment to make it happen, whether in our family, our
neighbourhood, or in the wider world. Every religious tradition speaks a great deal about 'peace' and in Lithuania, in
the eighteenth century, Rabbi Joel ben Abraham Shemariah
advocated the search for peace in these words:

Your first aim here on earth should to be at peace with
all people, Jew and non-Jew alike. Contend with no one.

Your home should be a place of quietness and happiness, where no harsh word is ever heard, but love, friendship, modesty and a spirit of gentleness and reverence rules at the time.

But this spirit must not end with the home. In your dealings with the world you must allow neither money nor ambition to disturb you. Forego your rights in matters of honour, if need be, and above all envy no one.

For the main thing is peace. Peace with the whole world.

Rabbi Joel ben Abraham Shemariah

To a certain extent these words have an old-fashioned ring. In our power-crazed societies they offer an alternative way. They also underline that the search for peace is tough going – in any age.

Spirit of God,
we thank you that you dance through creation,
scattering sparks of peace
– markers of healing,
in our wounded world.

When Will Justice Come?

Many people today, in all parts of the world, ask, 'When will justice come?'

There are endless debates and discussions and seminars and expensive global conferences reflecting on this and related questions. When I was working in South India, I asked myself this question many times. I still do.

One day in Chennai (formerly Madras), after a particularly wearying day in the heat and dust, I remembered the

old Greek saying whose source I have never discovered.
This is it. What a huge contemporary challenge it holds!

When
Will
Justice
Come?
Justice will come
When
Those of us
Who are not injured
Are as
Indignant
As
Those who are.

Lord, forgive my calculated efforts to serve you,
only when it is convenient for me to do so.
only in those places where it is safe to do so,
and only with those who make it easy to do so.

Joe Seremane of South Africa, in Lifelines

New World Orders

What do Indian street children, Japanese railway
workers, Brazilian farmers, Nepali dalits (the former 'un-
touchables'), and European political activists have in
common? All were among the 100,000 people at the
fourth World Social Forum in Mumbai (formerly Bombay)
discussing the theme 'Another world is possible'.

David Haslam, Guardian, 31 *January* 2004

As a believer in the collective power of ordinary people to
change situations, I followed with interest this meeting in

India. The World Social Forum, which was started a few years ago, is an alternative to the World Economic Forum which for many years has brought together the world's political, business and financial leaders.

Such meetings affirm that another economic system is beginning to emerge – the solidarity of a people's economy which embraces fair trade, co-operative ownership and democratic state control of basic services. Another is the increasing pressure for land reform in Brazil, India and elsewhere. This World Forum holds at its heart equality, justice and collective freedom, and, as one speaker noted, it is also about love – genuinely caring for each other in a wounded world.

These words of David Haslam inspire all of us who seek for a new world order:

At the WSF, women, indigenous people, street-children, disabled people, dalits and others victimised by the present world system are at the centre. The WSF does not claim to be another world, but that another world is possible. That aspiration is at the heart of Jesus's message, in his teaching about the kingdom of God, and would also ring bells in other faith communities. People of faith should engage with the WSF process, they would add an additional spiritual dimension.

David Haslam, Guardian, *31 January 2004*

Mother and Father of all,
may I live this day
in solidarity with
Indian street children,
Japanese railway workers,
Brazilian farmers,
Nepali dalits
and European political activists,
believing with them in a new world order.

Detention

This letter from Cheikh Kone from the Ivory Coast reflects the situation of many of our sisters and brothers in the world.

During the Presidential elections in the Ivory Coast, the ruling party decided to manipulate the results. I and some other journalists, wanting to tell the truth, wrote and published articles criticising the regime.

The information was leaked to the military. They contacted my family, and it was clear that my life was on the line. In a state of panic I phoned my dad and my brother-in-law. They both strongly advised me to flee the country.

From that time I had a price on my head. I had to leave, if not for my own sake, then for my family who could also suffer violence because of the articles.

I crossed the border to Ghana, then to Benin by road. Then to South Africa where I stayed for six weeks near the docks – just living on the roadside. One day I stowed away on a ship because I could not risk staying on in S. Africa. I did not know where the ship was going.

After spending nine days and nights without food and water, I was discovered by the crew. They told me the ship was going to Australia.

A day after arriving, I was woken up by two uniformed men who asked me, 'Who told you to come to this country? Don't you know that you will go to prison for 10 years.' They then threatened me, blackmailed me, and told me I was a liar. I had yet to set foot on Australian soil.

After this introduction I was taken to Port Hedland detention centre where I am now.

From a personal letter

God of the dispossessed,
show me how I can be in touch
with people like Cheikh Kone
who is without a home
because he spoke the truth.

Sparrows in Rafah

Alison, a former chemistry teacher who lives in a small village in the Scottish Highlands, is a long-time friend. She is a quiet, self-effacing person, yet in recent years Alison has been part of an international peace team in Rafah in Gaza monitoring the demolition of homes by the Israeli army. Not only has she seen terrible violence against the local Palestinian people, but she has also witnessed the death of a fellow peace-worker by the Israeli bulldozers as they demolished homes.

Having been in Israel/Palestine, I realize that the situation is complex and that there is great suffering on both sides of this seemingly insoluble conflict. Any peace plan needs international support, and yet we cannot ignore the mountain of human suffering which at the present time covers the land of Christ's birth and ministry.

On a regular basis, Alison sends back accounts of her experiences in Rafah where over two thousand homes have been demolished for security reasons. Many local people, including women and children, have been killed. Hundreds have been injured. Every night in Rafah is accompanied by the melody of machine-gun fire interspersed with random louder bangs from tank shells, flares or occasional bombs, and that melody is sometimes continued in the day.

In one of her reports, Alison holds together this massive human agony with the nest-building of the local sparrows. As I read her words, I felt that they were a meditation for our whole world in which pain and hope constantly intermingle.

Standing as a human shield between the tanks, watch-towers and municipal workers as they repaired water and sewage pipes broken by bulldozer action, I had plenty of time to contemplate the arid rubble-strewn wasteland created by Israel, and to marvel at the resilience of the sparrows making use of the shell-hole nest-boxes in the still standing building.

No-man's land, on closer inspection, contains not only the pathetic remains of family homes but also traces of beans and other crops from gardens and farms that used to be places of fertility and abundance in this area. Even amidst this scene of desolation 'the desert blooms'. New shoots in the rubble and debris. And the sparrows feed their young in the improvised nesting-boxes un-aware of the nightmare which surrounds their quiet shelter.

Alison Phillips, in Comment *(the news magazine of Highland*
Perthshire), vol. 23, no. 5

Taming the Gospel

Jock Dalrymple was for many years a Catholic priest in Edinburgh. He was also a prolific writer, retreat-giver and popular preacher. A man of many dimensions, with a real understanding of our often fragile human condition. Many mourned his passing. His was a prophetic voice – always confronting the institutional church when it tended to become absorbed in its own domestic agendas.

But what made Jock very special in the eyes of many was his ability to walk alongside folk who found themselves on the margins of society. And he always walked 'with them' – aware of his own vulnerability, and theirs. His home was a place of welcome for many who found themselves out in the storm. In him, the broken knew they had a friend.

In one of his books, Jock warned his readers about 'taming the Gospel'. It's an insight that is much needed today. If we go too far in 'taming' the truth of Christ we lose the vision altogether. He wrote:

We are just beginning to get away from the idea that holiness consists in prayer and charity and abstention from politics. You can only go so far in taming the Gospel. If you persist in removing its disturbing elements, you wake up one day to find that you have lost the Christian vision altogether.

Jock Dalrymple, Simple Prayer

Challenging God,
may we follow you into the hard places
of political involvement:
of making our voice heard in the market place,
of refusing to tame your gospel
in a world of easy compromise.

Part Eight

Searching for an Authentic Spirituality

Christian life is not just a question of getting through our lives; every word of the New Testament suggests to us that it is of supreme importance that we live our lives in a state of continuous expansion of heart and spirit, growing in love and becoming more firmly rooted in God.

John Main, The Joy of Being

Columba's Legacy

> Love bears all things, believes all things, hopes all things, endures all things.

> I Corinthians 13.7

In 1997 there were celebrations on Iona to mark the death of Columba, 1,400 years earlier, in 597. In a sermon at that time, Norman Shanks, then leader of the Iona Community, spoke of Columba's legacy.

There is so much to treasure in the heritage of Columba and the Celtic tradition. The scholars may debate the details, but the main thrusts and themes are beyond dispute.

What was distinctive was not only Columba's holiness; there was also a wholeness, a roundness and rootedness about his faith. His life was grounded in the conviction that God's loving purpose encompasses and permeates the whole of life, is relevant to every human need and situation; and that is why the Gospel is literally 'good news'.

God is to be discovered, experienced, encountered not only in contemplative tranquillity, not only in remote, beautiful Hebridean Islands; but also in the hurly-burly of life, in corporate worship, in the ebb and flow of relationships, in grappling with the struggles, tensions and issues of the day.

Contrary to what is often perceived and purveyed as 'Celtic Christianity', often self-indulgent, essentially individualistic, the true Columban tradition is about engagement not escape. It holds spiritual and social concerns inextricably together. It is indeed a rich legacy, a formidable challenge for those who seek to walk in the footsteps of Columba today.

Norman Shanks, 'Engagement not escape',
sermon preached in Iona Abbey in 1997

O Trinity of Love,
you have been with us at the world's beginning;
be with us till the world's end.
You have been with us at our life's shaping;
be with us at our life's end.
You have been with us at the sun's rising;
be with us till the day's end.

Based on a Gaelic prayer

Teresa's Truth

Christ has no body on earth but yours;
yours are the only hands
with which he can do his work,
yours are the only feet
with which he can go about the world,
yours are the only eyes
through which his compassion
can shine forth upon a troubled world.
Christ has no body on earth but yours.

Teresa of Avila

When I first heard the famous prayer of Teresa of Avila I did not grasp its meaning. I understood the words in the prayer but its deeper truth bypassed me. Looking back, I think the reason for this was because I believed in a God who was somehow doing most of his own work on earth, and only used us humans from time to time. I accept it was a strange belief, but not an uncommon one.

How could we really be 'Christ's body' in this world? Surely God in all of his power and glory was not depending on a person like myself to be a 'co-creator' as a Jewish prayer puts it?

It was when I went to my first parish in the East End of Glasgow that I began to read these words in a different way. In that area where there were many markers of social deprivation, I saw everyday, ordinary folk doing the work of Jesus Christ! They had no dog-collars round their necks, or any formal training in theology, but it was certainly through their eyes that Christ's compassion shone out on these poor streets. Of that I had no doubt. I may not have been the body of Christ on earth, but they certainly were! Teresa's words, written all these years earlier, rang true.

The Unstoppable Journey

> When you seek God, seek him in your heart. He is not in Jerusalem, not in Mecca nor in the Hajj.
>
> *Yunus Emre (1280–1330)*

In one of his encyclicals, Pope John Paul talks at length about the modern search for meaning and for a sense of the transcendent. He calls this search for meaning an 'unstoppable journey' and enlarges on this in a way which has helped my own search. Many of the people I meet know that they are on this kind of journey, even if they are unsure of its details. What they do know is that they are travelling, sometimes too slowly and sometimes too fast!

It emerges that men and women are on a journey of discovery which is humanly unstoppable – a search for truth and a search for a person to whom they might entrust themselves.

In different cultures, the fundamental questions which pervade human life arise: Who am I? Where have I come from and where am I going? Why is there evil and suffering? What is there after this life? These questions are found in the sacred writings of Israel, and also in the Veda and Avesta; in the writings of Confucius and Lse-Tse; in the preachings of Tirthankara and Buddha; they appear in the poetry of Homer and in the tragedies of Euripides and Sophocles; in the philosophical works of Plato and Aristotle.

The church is no stranger to this journey of discovery, nor could it ever be. Having received the gift of the ultimate truth about human life through the Paschal mystery, the church has a duty to be a partner in humanity's shared struggle to arrive at a truth while also proclaiming its own certitudes, though with a sense that every truth attained is but a step towards that fullness of truth which will appear in the final revelation of God.

Pope John Paul II, from the encyclical Fides et Ratio

I stand at the door and knock. If you respond to my voice and open the door, I will enter your space and share your food: and you will share with me.

Revelation 3.20

The Journey Ahead

Love was without beginning, is and shall be without ending.

Julian of Norwich (1342–1420)

Kate McIlhagga was a member of the Iona Community and a minister in the United Reformed Church. Many people, including myself, found in Kate both a faithful friend and an insightful spiritual guide. Her death some years ago was widely mourned, but her poems and reflections live on in many hearts around the world. In her own life she had experienced joy and sorrow, perhaps in equal measure, but even in her last illness, Kate understood that life was a journey, in which the travelling and the arrival were both important.

She was a true pilgrim and her prayers speak of many kinds of pilgrimages, both inner and outer. They are imbued with a Celtic understanding of the Christian faith, and this particular prayer is one to which I often return. Kate walked in wonder and moved to the surging of the Spirit, always seeking to travel in patterns of God's making. She also knew that when this earthly journey ended, a new one in Christ was about to begin.

> Bless, O God,
> the journey ahead.
> Bless the travelling
> and the arrival.
> Bless those who welcome
> and those
> who receive hospitality,
> that
> Christ

may
come
among
us
in
journeying
and
in
stillness.

Kate McIlhagga

The Comforter

When the day of Pentecost came, all the believers were gathered together in one place. Suddenly there was a noise from the sky which sounded like a strong wind blowing, and it filled the whole house where they were sitting. They were all filled with the Holy Spirit, and began to talk in other languages, as the Spirit enabled them to speak.

Acts 2.1–4

Jürgen Moltmann's theological writings have enabled me to enlarge my knowledge of the Gospels. In his many books he helps his readers to penetrate a little of the mystery of God, of Christ and of the Holy Spirit. When he gave the well-known Lambeth Lecture in London he called his talk 'Pentecost and Theology of Life'.

In that lecture, he spoke at length about the Holy Spirit. In the second chapter of Acts, we are told that the outpouring of the Spirit was the mark of God's creative power at work in our lives and in the world. Where the Holy Spirit is, God is present in a special way, and for Moltmann one of the most beautiful names for this liberating Spirit is 'the Comforter'.

As we pray for the coming of the Spirit, we open ourselves to the energy of God flowing through our lives. Even when we hardly know what to pray for, God's Spirit, already at work in our lives, helps us – a truth made strongly by Paul when he was writing to the community of believers in Rome (Romans 8.26).

And about 'the Comforter' Moltmann says this:

> Whoever prays for the Holy Spirit to come to us, into our hearts, into our community and to our earth, does not want to flee to heaven or be removed to the great beyond. Magnificent, unbroken affirmation of life lies behind our prayers for the Spirit to come to us fragile and earthly human beings.

Comforter and Source of Life, attune us to your purposes for all creation.

Humanity's Longing

At the time of the first Gulf War in 1991, Michael Hare Duke was working as a bishop in the Episcopal Church in Scotland.

With many others he was horrified at the events which were unfolding in the Gulf, but he also recognized that war releases powerful emotions that bring many people to prayer. They want to discover a power for good equal to the destructiveness unleashed by conflict. That raises many questions. 'Where is God at such a time?' 'Does "right" in the end prevail?' 'How can we pray at a time of war?'

In response to these and other questions, Michael edited a small book, *Praying for Peace: Reflections on the Gulf crisis*, which included contributions from women and men of all faiths. He was anxious to draw on the spiritual traditions of all humanity, and to explore a common ground for peacemaking. At the time I found it a wonderfully helpful book, and this short piece from his introduction seems as relevant now as in the early 1990s.

Beyond the present crisis is the wider threat to our whole world. Many [of those who have shared their thoughts in this book] link together the energy of prayer with action for justice. They reflect a way of love which in a dark time can light a candle of hope. Most importantly they are a witness to the great longing for humanity to discover a new dynamic of peacemaking. Peace belongs to people and will be sustained by everyone's united goodwill. It requires a willingness to share the limited resources of a world which can no longer afford to make competition between individuals and nations the main thrust of its way of life. If that is to be possible it will require a revolution within ourselves and a surrender of our power to the authority of God; that too is what prayer is about.

Michael Hare Duke, ed., Praying for Peace: Reflections on the Gulf crisis

God of ancient calm

God of ancient calm
let
your
peace
still
us.

God of fearful storm
fill
us
with
awe.

God of mountains
widen
our
vision.

God of shing stars
illumine
our
journey.

God of lonely plains
touch
these
empty
spaces
within
us
where
we
are
vulnerable
enough
to
meet
you.

Unscathed, Unscarred

Angie Andrews is a member of a Christian community in Brisbane, which over many years has lived alongside individuals and families on the edge of society. The community's prophetic witness has been an inspiration to many of us, far beyond Australia's shores. This is one of Angie's poems, rooted in her life of compassionate outreach.

There is precious little acceptance in our society
of the changes in our bodies,
brought about by sacrifice,
by the giving of life to others.
People want us to look
unscathed,
unscarred,
without the
sagging breasts,
without the
stretch-marks in our stomach,
without the line
of strain and struggle.
We are to look ageless, timeless,
the image of the lithe and slender.

Where is the place of beauty
derived from love
and developed through sacrifice?

Where are the people who will celebrate
the signs of someone who has given themselves
to others
through touch and tears and love
unnumbered times?

Who of you will join me
in the risk of being worn out,
of being wrinkled,
of being thrown away?

We are not fools
who give what we cannot keep
to gain what we cannot lose.

Angie Andrews, in Dorothy Millar, Seeds for the Morrow

A Mellow Heart

As I come
to a peaceful awareness
of my limited grasp of truth,
I don't need to defend myself
against people or experiences
which might hold new
or challenging information.
I become open to these truths
that reside
half-hidden,
and often surprising,
in my own
and others' journeys.
And this is a gift
– a rare treasure
freeing me to understand
rather than be understood;
calling me
to fewer words,
to awareness,
to humility
to patience,

> to laughter,
> to tenderness,
> to listening,
> to dancing in the rain,
> to waiting on that God
> who always
> welcomes home
> a mellow heart.

Peter Millar, in Waymarks

An Ancient Prayer

> Now the message that we have heard from his Son and
> announce is this: God is light, and there is no darkness
> at all in him. If, then, we say that we have fellowship
> with him, yet at the same time live in the darkness, we
> are lying both in our words and actions.

1 John 1.5–6

Later in this passage we are given the assurance of Christ's
forgiveness if we can truly repent of our failures. Yet that
movement from our own limitations into the 'marvellous
light' of God is a daily one – a continuing one, and I am
always suspicious of those who feel that they have it 'all
right' with Jesus! Sometimes such a conviction actually
lets us off the hook in a way which is contrary to gospel
teaching.

For my own part, I like this ancient prayer from Iran
which expresses well our often faltering human condition.

> All that we ought to have thought,
> and have not thought;
> all that we ought to have said,
> and have not said;

all that we ought to have done,
and have not done;
pray we, O God, for forgiveness.

All that we ought not to have thought,
and yet have thought;
all that we ought not to have spoken,
and yet have spoken;
all that we ought not to have done,
and yet have done;
for thoughts, words and works,
pray we, O God, for forgiveness.

Prayer from Iran

Don't Hide

Don't hide:
don't run,
but rather
discover in the
midst of fragmentation
a new way forward
a different kind of journey
marked by its fragility,
uncertainty
and lack of definition.
And on that path
to hold these hands
that even in their brokenness
create a new tomorrow.

To dance on the margins,
and to see
the face of Christ
where hurt
is real
and pain a way of life.

To be touched
in the eye of the storm,
aware that tomorrow
may not bring peace.

Impossible, you say;
let me retreat
and find my rest.

What rest, my friend
in these fragmented times?

A Living Church

If the Lord does not build the house, the work of the builders is useless.

Psalm 127. 1

Almost forty years ago the theologian Charles Davis left the Roman Catholic Church which he had served as a priest for twenty years. One year later he wrote his influential book *A Question of Conscience*. In this book he deals with why he left the church, and outlines the kind of radical reforms he believes are necessary in the structures of all churches if they are to connect authentically with people's lives.

Looking back, some of his words were prophetic. Since the 1960s a huge number of people who had a church connection have ceased to be part of institutional religion. There are many reasons for this, and countless books have been written on the subject. Perhaps too many! However, these words of Davis still need to be heeded. He reminds us that institutional structures have often been rejected by people who remain committed to the Christian faith, but who have discovered that these structures are in themselves barriers to spiritual growth and to the deepening of their faith in Christ. He wrote:

> To continue to play the present institutional game within and across the denominational structures is to hinder the coming into full visibility of a radically different and better form of Christian presence in the world. Our churches do not recognise that it is often a person's Christian faith which leads them to reject institutional structures inimical to the self-understanding and freedom of the individual and to Christian truth and love.

Charles Davis, A Question of Conscience

Lord,
walk with those who love you,
but find institutional religion
difficult to handle.

All Shall Be Well

All shall be well, and all shall be well,
and all manner of things shall be well.

Julian of Norwich

When the world was different,
Julian
wrote these words
from her place of prayer.

The centuries have gone,
and still her
quiet words
echo
in the heart.

Through
wars,
famine
and
abandonment
her
quiet words
echo
in the heart.

All will
be well, she said,
and,
against all the odds,
all manner of things
WILL BE WELL.

The Lord will protect you from all danger;
He will keep you safe.
He will protect you as you come and go,
now and for ever.

Psalm 121.7–8

Part Nine

Encountering God's Surprises

You saw that we were only human . . .

Our grace embodied
with clay feet

Our beauty
with its flaws

Our longing
still searching for its source

Our lives
so very raw

Our compassion
wounded still

. . . And you loved us all the more!

Noel Davies, Love Finds a Way

Warp and Weft Glimpsed

When I was warden of Iona Abbey I used to be spellbound by the ever-changing, often stormy, waters of the Sound of Iona which lies between the island of Iona and the neighbouring, much larger Isle of Mull.

The writer Jan Sutch Pickard, who some years later held the same post at the Abbey, has gloriously articulated the connection between these restless waters and our life within the Iona Community in one of her beautifully crafted poems.

> On a still December day,
> Warp and weft glimpsed
> In the gold threads of the dawn sky,
> In the blue-grey restless waters of the Sound,
> In our laughter and tears,
> In our life together in this place –
> Your mysterious weaving of the world.

> *Jan Sutch Pickard,* Out of Iona:
> Words from a crossroads of the world

Jan's weaving together of nature, human experience and life within a modern religious community also mirrors something of Celtic Christianity's belief of the interconnectedness of spirit and matter. Some traditional words that have come down to us from the islands off Scotland's west coast remind us of this reality:

> I believe, O Lord and God of the peoples,
> That Thou art the creator of the high heavens,
> That Thou art the creator of the skies above,

That Thou art the creator of the oceans below,
That Thou created my body from dust and ashes,
Gave to my body breath,
And to my soul its possession.

From Esther De Waal, ed., The Celtic Vision:
Prayers and blessings from the Outer Hebrides

Goodnight God

Goodnight God,
I hope that
you are having
a good time
being the world.

I like the world very much.
I'm glad you made the plants
and trees and
rain and summers.

When the summer is nearly over
the leaves begin to fall.
I hope you have a good time
being the world.

I like how God feels around
everyone in the world.

God, I am very happy that
I live on you.

Your arms clasp
around the world.

I like you
and your friends.

Every time I open my eyes
I see the gleaming sun.

I like the animals
and us creatures of the world.

I love my dear friends.

*Some words written by a young boy called Danu, in
Elizabeth Roberts and Elias Amidon, eds.,* Earth Prayers

In South Chicago

When living in South Chicago, an Afro-American friend
told me one day that earlier in the week he had been asked
for some money by a homeless person. The lowest note he
had was five dollars so he gave that. A few minutes later,
the same guy came back to him. (Had he not had enough?)
But much to his amazement the homeless man told my
friend that he had gone to get change of the five dollars,
and handed him back four dollars!

GOD OF EACH ENCOUNTER

Help us to

Live

IN SUCH A WAY

So that

When
UPSIDE-DOWN
Things

          Happen

    We

       Can

       CELEBRATE

   And

       Go

          On

     Our

       Way

      REJOICING!

Barry's Note

Barry is a good, mildly eccentric friend who lives in Melbourne where he works as a journalist. Over the years I have found many of his articles inspiring, not least because he has a vibrant sense of humour. That humour is linked to spiritual wisdom, and an email from Barry often brightens my day! This particular note – written not long after the birth of his daughter – reveals much about our universal search for love, laughter, goodness and God.

Dear Peter

It's all happening:
the usual joys,
the unusual surprises
and the tolerable woes
– the human condition
sprawled out on the lounge floor,
tickling his daughter's toes,
begging a cup of coffee of the missus,

and thanking Christ
for light and love.

Speak soon

Barry

God of unusual surprises,
For toes that need to be tickled
And for Dads who tickle them
And for Mums who bring the coffee
While the toes are being tickled
We really are thankful.

The Prodigal's Brother

There have been thousands of interpretations of the story of the prodigal son.

Helder Camara, who was Archbishop of Olinda and Recife in North-East Brazil and who identified his ministry with the lives of the poorest, wrote many poetic reflections, over a period of fifty years.

This one on the prodigal son's elder brother reflects his conviction that everyone on earth carries within them something of the Creator's living mark.

I pray incessantly
for the conversion
of the prodigal son's
brother.

Ever in my ear
rings the dread warning:
'the one has awoken

from his life of sin,
when will the other
awaken
from his virtue?'

Dom Helder Camara, A Thousand Reasons for Living.

Spirit of Life –
awaken me
from being too pious,
from easy judgements of the other,
and from a failure to recognize
that actually the mote is in my own eye
a lot of the time.

Rabbi Susya

In his interesting book *Through the Labyrinth* (Penguin USA, 1993), which is about the different spiritual journeys people make in life, Peter Occhiogrosso quotes a Hasidic rabbi named Susya. Susya's words are succinct: 'When I die no one is going to ask me why I wasn't Moses. They're going to ask me why I wasn't Susya.'

One of the things which has always attracted me to the Gospels is the fact that when Jesus meets people he values them as they are – not as others imagine them to be, or even as they imagine themselves. An obvious example of this is in his rather surprising encounter (at least to others) in Jericho with the highly unpopular tax-collector Zacchaeus (Luke 19). Jesus sees so much possibility in this particular person whom others despise.

And we are told that when Zacchaeus recovered from his own surprise of being spoken to by Jesus, he hurried down from the tree from which he was watching the proceedings and welcomed him with 'great joy' – not a quality which had been too much in evidence to the locals prior to this day! In that moment of meeting, Zacchaeus touched into his real self, and allowed the good qualities in his character to emerge.

So often we don't like ourselves enough to be ourselves. We may feel that if we were true to who we actually are under our many social masks, we might be rejected or laughed at or even despised. We fear exposure. So did Zacchaeus until the day he met Jesus. Then he felt free to be himself.

> *Thank you, Lord, that you know me as I really am,*
> *and that I need not be afraid to be*
> *true to my deepest self.*

Memories

It's the hug,
It's the crazy joke,
It's the warm hand,
It's the fish and chips.

It's the sudden laughter,
It's the silent tears,
It's the high noon,
It's the mobile phone.

It's the broken bikes,
It's the washing up,
It's the school run,
It's the touch of love.

It's the dog's lick,
It's the loud music,
It's the magic smiles,
It's the stupid dancing.

It's the screaming kids,
It's the tender note,
It's the burnt toast,
It's the midnight kiss.

It's the hidden pain,
It's the long search,
It's the truth-telling,
It's the healing.

It's the intimacy,
It's the parting,
It's the tears,
It's the farewell.

It's life,
It's death
It's the Spirit
Of blessing.

It's the God
Of surprises
Met again
On the journey.

Keep Me Reasonably Sweet

Lord, you know better than myself that I am growing older and will some day be old. Keep me from being talkative and particularly from the fatal habit of thinking that I must say something on every subject and on every occasion.

Release me from craving to straighten out everybody's affairs. Make me thoughtful but not moody; helpful but not bossy. With my vast store of wisdom, it seems a pity not to use it all, but you know, Lord, that I want a few friends at the end. Keep my mind from the recital of endless details – give me wings to come to the point.

I ask for grace enough to listen to the tales of others' pain. But seal my lips on my own aches and pains – they are increasing, and my love of rehearsing them is becoming sweeter as the years go by. Help me to endure them with patience.

I dare not ask for improved memory but for a growing humility and a lessening cocksureness when my memory seems to clash with the memories of others. Teach me the glorious lessen that occasionally it is possible that I may be mistaken.

Keep me be reasonably sweet. I do not want to be a saint – some of them are so hard to live with – but a sour old woman is one of the crowning works of the devil.

Give me the ability to see good things in unexpected places, and talents in unexpected people. And give me, O Lord, the grace to tell them so.

Attributed to a seventeenth-century nun

A Korean Vision

In a few moments of quiet stillness as we seek to be in touch with our inner-self, we can be strengthened by the vision of God's presence in the world contained in this Korean prayer, written by Marion Kim.

Like the seed
that grows into a tree
open our eyes
to the new vision
as green leaf sprouts
awaken to the blue sky.

Nurture
in us
the sunlight and rain
of your truth.

Make us strong
like the tall tree
with leafy branches
mothering
those who
need protection from
the storms of poverty and injustice.

O Holy Spirit
make us one with you:
deepen our roots
in nature, history and culture
and breathe into us
your healing power
to reach beyond the barriers of division
and create a new community
of love and peace.

Korean prayer

Simeon

Led by the Spirit, Simeon went into the Temple. When the parents brought the child Jesus into the Temple, to do for him what the Law required, Simeon took the child in his arms and gave thanks to God:

Now Lord, you have kept your promise,
    and you may let your servant go in peace.
With my own eyes I have seen your salvation
    which you have prepared in the presence of all
        peoples;
a light to reveal you to the nations,
    and to bring glory to your people Israel.

Luke 2.27–32

> Simeon,
> you waited
> with an open heart:
> an ordinary guy,
> living in Jerusalem
> who longed
> for God's ways
> to be seen in the city.
>
> And one day
> God surprised you
> away beyond
> all your imaginings
> when you took
> that child in your arms
> right there in the Temple.

And you knew
in an instant,
that God had come
in a special way
to transform the world
and yourself.

Genesis 12.1–9

The Lord said to Abram, 'Leave your native land, your
relatives and your father's home, and go to a country
that I am going to show you. I will give you many
descendants, and they will become a great nation. I will
bless you and make your name famous, so that you will
be a blessing.

Genesis 12.1–2

Any journeying of the kind Abram was asked to undertake
involves risk-taking. Moving into the unknown, both in an
outer and inner sense, throws our life into a new space – a
place which is often scary. I know I experienced that after
Dorothy's very sudden death. A new path lay ahead in my
own life, but it seemed full of uncertainties and unknowns.
Many of the old markers were gone.

It's obvious that the more secure we feel in our present
situation, the more we avoid taking risks. Why change
when it's all relatively OK? There must have been something of that feeling in Abram's mind. The Bible notes that
when he actually started out from Haran as the Lord had
told him to do, he was in fact 75 years old! Long past 65,
and well into his pension.

Yet he got up and began the long haul, along with a
whole retinue of others. They were on the way to Canaan.
Yet what seems significant in all of this obvious risk-taking

was the assurance that they did not travel alone. They were held in the embrace of God. That's what made it possible. And so it is with us.

> *God of Abraham,*
> *surprise us,*
> *turn us upside-down,*
> *take away the known markers,*
> *even if just from time to time!*

New Every Morning

> Blessed art Thou,
> O Lord our God,
> King of the Universe,
> who creates the world
> every morning afresh.

Jewish prayer

This evocative prayer reminds us both of the glory of God and of the fresh possibilities of each new day. The day that is God's day for us. The Psalmist wrote of proclaiming the Lord's greatness, and then continued that theme in these memorable words: 'Every day I will thank you: I will praise you for ever and ever' (Psalm 145.1–3).

And in the teaching of Jesus we read that it is no good worrying about what the day may or may not hold for us. Rather, our main concern should be that we are open to the various movements of God's Spirit within us. That does not mean that the new day will be free of pain or disappointment, but I think it underlies the truth that whatever situation we are in, we are not alone. Every morning

Christ knocks at the door of our heart and awakens us again to the realities and wonder of the living God.

And sometimes a short prayer can open up the new day for us in a special way. There are two prayers which are used in the worship in Iona Abbey which always put me in a fresh place, so to speak, as a new day begins. One is a Mexican prayer, and the other comes from the Syrian church. These prayers have very different origins, but they help us to place a frame of meaning around the hours that lie ahead. They also connect us to our sisters and brothers around the world who may be half way through their day, or sound asleep on some distant continent!

> Lord,
> If this day you have to correct us,
> Put us right not out of anger
> But with a mother and father's love.
> So may we, your children,
> Be kept free of falseness and foolishness.

From the Mexican church

> Lord, open to us today the sea of your mercy
> And water us with full streams
> From the riches of your grace
> And the springs of your kindness.
> Make us children of quietness and heirs of peace . . .
> Strengthen our weakness by your power,
> And bind us close to you and to each other.

From the Syrian church

Seven Hard-working Days

When Nick Midgley wrote this he was 13. That was some years back. I don't know if Nick still values what he wrote then, but I do!

> On the first day God made light,
> And he was dazzled and made dark,
> And then a switch.
>
> On the second day God made the earth
> And he took the elements,
> Shuffled them,
> And dealt them.
>
> On the third day God made plants.
> He learnt to breathe the fresh air
> Before it was too late,
> And he saw beauty.
>
> On the fourth day God made the stars
> And God was proud of them.
> He winked at them
> And they winked back.
>
> On the fifth day God made birds and fish
> And wanted conversation,
> But they would not talk.
>
> On the sixth morn he made animals to talk to
> But they wouldn't listen,
> And in the evening he made man.
> He said, 'Man, my companion',
> And man said, 'Off my land,
> You're trespassing'.

On the seventh day God rested
And thought.
And he never saw the eighth day.

Nick Midgley, quoted in Donald Hilton, Liturgy of Life

The Ultimate Referee

It is in times of crisis that prayers are usually most heartfelt, and nowhere more so than among football fans at a European Championship – like the one in Portugal in 2004.

After drawing against Switzerland, Croatian fans petitioned the Virgin Mary at the famous shrine at Fatima. The results of that are still unclear.

In Germany, meanwhile, the pessimism was such about the national team that the popular daily, *Bild*, printed a prayer beginning: 'Dear Football God, let the other teams be even worse than us . . .'

Much more dignified and sporting was a prayer by Archbishop Werner Thissen of Hamburg, published in a local church paper. The Archbishop, an ardent fan himself, prayed that the best team would win the tournament.

He asked bosses to turn a blind eye to staff who appeared at work in the morning with 'square eyes'. An extra portion of patience was sought for wives faced with football-obsessed men and, he added, may the game produce fantastic play with 'first-class goals'.

'Lord, I depend on you as the great and merciful referee,' the prayer concluded, and 'let us in Europe deal with each other fairly, not only in football'.

All sides can say Amen to that, but was the Almighty looking with favour on the German team?

Part Ten

Being Open to the Moment

This
is
God's
day
so
make
the
most
of
it!

Words seen on a church poster

An African Creed

We believe in one High God, who out of love created the beautiful world and everything good in it. He created people and wanted them to be happy in the world. God loves the world and every nation and tribe on the earth. We have known this High God in the darkness, and now we know him in the light. God promised in the book of his word, the Bible, that he would save the world and all nations and tribes.

We believe that God, made good his promise by sending his son, Jesus Christ, a man in the flesh, a Jew by tribe, born poor in a little village, who left his home and was always on safari doing good, curing people by the power of God, teaching about God and showing that the meaning of religion is love. He was rejected by his people, tortured and nailed hands and feet to a cross, and died. He lay buried in the grave, but the hyenas did not touch him, and on the third day, he rose from the grave. He ascended to the skies. He is the Lord.

We believe that all our sins are forgiven through him. All who have faith in him must be sorry for their sins, be baptized in the Holy Spirit of God, live the rules of love and share the bread together in love, to announce the good news to others until Jesus comes again. We are waiting for him. He is alive. He lives. This we believe. Amen.

This African Creed was included in Vincent J. Donovan,
Christianity Rediscovered: An epistle from the Masai

The Wind of the Spirit

And Jesus said:
'The wind blows wherever it wishes.
You hear the sound it makes,
but you do not know where it comes from
or where it is going.
It is like that
with
everyone
who
is
born
of the Spirit.'

John 3.8

God of the wild Spirit,
help me,
for just
once in my life,
to take a risk
for You,
even if it is
a small one,
or
one all hedged around
with safety nets,
so that I can at least
start to understand
the words you spoke
to those
who wanted security
rather that Life.

God's Timing?

In the Old Testament, the book of Ecclesiastes contains the thoughts of 'the Philosopher', a person who reflected deeply on how short and contradictory human life is, with its mysterious injustices and frustrations and concluded that life is useless. He could not understand the ways of God.

Yet in spite of this, he advised people to work hard, and to enjoy the gifts of God as much and as long as they could. The fact that his thoughts appear negative and sometimes downright depressing, shows that biblical faith is well able to take into account pessimism and doubt in human nature.

> Everything that happens in this world
> happens at the time God chooses.

He sets the time for birth
and the time for death.

> The time for planting
> and the time for pulling up.

> The time for destroying
> and the time for healing.

The time for tearing down
and the time for building up.

The time for sorrow and the time for joy

The time for mourning and the time for dancing

The time for making love and the time for not making
love.

The time for kissing and the time for not kissing.

The time for finding and the time for losing.

The time for saving and the time for throwing away.

The time for tearing and the time for mending.
The time for silence and the time for talk.
The time for love and the time for hate.
The time for war and the time for peace.

Ecclesiastes 3.1–8

As One Unknown

If a soul is seeking God, its beloved is seeking it still more.

St John of the Cross (1542–91)

Since his death in 1965, many writers have been critical of the work and writings of the missionary doctor and Nobel Laureate Albert Schweitzer. During his lifetime, through his medical work in the hospital at Lamberene in Gabon he became world famous, but as early as 1906 when he published his *The Quest of the Historical Jesus* he was known as a great theologian.

I continue to be attracted by words which he wrote in that book almost a century ago. They sum up the nature of our continuing quest for the Jesus of history who is also the Christ of faith. They speak to our technological age as much as they did at the start of the twentieth century.

He comes to us as One unknown, without a name, as of old, by the lake-side. He came to those people who knew him not. He speaks to us the same word; 'Follow thou me!' and sets us to the tasks which He has to fulfill for our time.

He commands. And to those who obey Him, whether they be wise or simple, He will reveal Himself in the toils, the conflicts, the sufferings which they shall pass through in His fellowship, and, as an ineffable mystery, they shall learn in their own experience, Who he is.'

Albert Schweitzer, The Quest of the Historical Jesus

> *Known, yet unknown,*
> *without a name*
> *yet holding every name.*
> *In the mystery of love*
> *you come to us*
> *and in tenderness*
> *reveal the meaning of our lives*
> *and the pattern of our days.*

The Wideness of God's Mercy

Jim is a friend who has travelled the world, experienced many personal triumphs and tragedies and sometimes finds watching the nightly TV news not one of life's more encouraging experiences. Despite that, or because of it, he goes the extra mile for literally dozens of folk.

Dear Jim

I understand why you get depressed about the state of the world! Listening to the news today, every item seemed to be about violence and turmoil. Yet I also remember that millions and millions of people are just getting on with their lives in quiet ordinariness – and in our strange times that's a miracle.

The other day, one of my more cynical neighbours, whose friendship is special, was carrying on with some light banter, when quite suddenly he became more serious and said to me, 'What does your God make of all of this anarchy in the world?' I immediately pointed out that he was not 'my' God, but having said that, I thought about a midrash which Jewish rabbis often tell.

When the people of Israel had miraculously crossed the Red Sea and their pursuers met their watery death, the guardian angels in heaven, like their human counterparts on earth, were celebrating – singing and dancing. The evil ones had been vanquished. Then gradually they noticed that God was not joining in this merriment but was quietly weeping. Puzzled they asked God, 'Are you not pleased that your people have been saved and delivered from tyranny? Why are you sad' God answered them, 'How can I celebrate? My children are also drowning.'

That emphasizes that we're not the only ones sad about all the turmoil around. In the wideness of his mercy, God also weeps.

Keep in touch.

Peter

These Three Remain

Meantime,
  these
    three
      remain . . .

        faith
         hope
          and love . . .

And the greatest of these

is love.

I Corinthians 13.13

Through the centuries, millions and millions of children, women and men from around our interconnected world have heard these words which Paul wrote to the early Church in Corinth.

And the truth is that they do remain.

Without their truth our essential humanity would be lost.

They are powerful words, but also strangely gentle.

Inviting and also profoundly challenging.

They hold both mystery and wisdom.

Timeless words.

Words of transformation for today – right where we are now.

Holy Spirit, give us faith,
Holy Spirit, give us hope,
Holy Spirit, give us love,
Revive your work in this land,
Beginning with me.

From Uganda

Held in Love

> The sovereign Lord, the holy God of Israel, says to the people, 'Come back and quietly trust in me. Then you will be strong and secure.'

Isaiah 30.15

This quiet evening prayer comes from Ghana in West Africa and reveals that depth of faith which characterizes the lives of African people. The prayer also places our daily living against the backcloth of the natural order.

We can read it slowly, remembering the ways in which our life, along with all of creation, is held in the Creator's purpose. As the prayer says, we need not fear the darkness of the night, for through the hours of sleep, One watches over us.

> The sun has disappeared,
> I have switched off the light,
> and my wife and children are asleep.
> The animals in the forest are full of fear,
> and so are the people on their mats.
> They prefer the day with your sun
> to the night.
> But I still know that
> your moon is there,
> and your eyes,
> and also your hands.
> Thus I am not afraid.
> This day again
> you led us wonder-fully.
> Everybody went to his mat
> satisfied and full.
> Renew us during sleep,

that in the morning
we may come afresh
to our daily jobs.
Be with our sisters and brothers
far away in Asia
who may be getting up now. Amen.

Prayer from Ghana

God of the Thorny Ground

I believe
in a God who shares with us
the thorny ground,
the desert
and all the uninviting places
where some of us have to live.

In a God
who suddenly weeps floods of tears,
with hands outstretched like a mother,
over my red and black village,
as he wept for his best friend
for death, for him.

I believe in a God
who never lets go,
never rests,
who is with me always
– even if we quarrel –
from one struggle
to the next,
as in a real battle.

A friend
and who is there with me
from coffee at daybreak,
until I sleep at night.

From 'A Labourer's Creed', Latin America

God in Every Path

The Lord says, 'When Babylonia's seventy years are over, I will show concern and keep my promise to bring you back home. Yes, I say, you will find me, and I will restore you to your land. I will gather you from every country and from every place to which I have scattered you, and I will bring you back to the land from which I had sent you away in exile.'

Jeremiah 29.1–14

The exiles were restless in Babylon. They longed for their homeland where they believed they could worship God in the only truly meaningful way. To some extent this was understandable, for Deuteronomy had made it impossible for a good Jew to live in an alien land.

The great legacy of Jeremiah is that he encouraged the people to rediscover the living God, not only in Jerusalem, but wherever they found themselves. God lets himself be found in Babylon: the 'unclean land' becomes the sphere of revelation. The Israelites can actually pray in Babylon, and find God's presence even in exile. Restoration would one day come, but meantime the living God was in their midst in a strange land and in a different culture.

One of the treasures handed down to us from the Celtic church is exactly this belief – that wherever we are, God is available! The mundane becomes the edge of glory. Our

journey in faith is never limited to a particular place or to
one way of worship. Rather, on hill, in hollow, on plain,
in sea and on every path, Christ is with us: his light
encircling our often uncertain journeying – a truth
expressed in this Celtic blessing:

> May God shield you on every steep.
> May Christ keep you in every path.
> May Spirit bathe you in every pass.

From Ether de Waal, ed., The Celtic Vision

A Tribal Elder's Forgiveness

Forgive each other. No conditions.

Those who abuse us, despise us, tear our children
from our bosom in the name of God –
Forgive them.

Those who rip us off, take all our possessions, our
    dignity, our land,
the loved animals of our place –
Forgive them.

Those who call us savage, ignorant pagan, inferior,
primitive, given to Spirit worship –
Forgive them.

Those who persecute us, annihilate our person,
lock us up in the name of justice, make us 'no one'
in our own land –
Forgive them.

Those who hurt us to our hearts, savage and wound
our every part so that we can never bring ourselves to
    forgive them –
Forgive them.

Those who desecrate our values and replace them with
    their gods of
greed, corruption, decimation –
Forgive them.

For if we do not forgive
then the same evil spirit
will enter into us and take us over.
Forgive. Forgive.
Forgive in the Spirit of the Cross of Life.

> *From the vast heart of compassion of a tribal elder,*
> *quoted in Noel Davies,* Campfire of the Heart

Salutation to the Dawn

Every day is precious. Every new morning brings with it
fresh possibilities. St Anthony of Padua spoke about this
poetically: 'Consider every day that you are for the first
time – as it were – beginning: and always act with the same
fervour as on the first day you began.'

Anthony's wisdom was rooted in his commitment to
Christ, but many other great writings express a similar
truth about the new day. These glorious words of 'salutation to the dawn' come from a Sanskrit prayer – a language with which I feel a close affinity for my daughter
Sulekha who was born in India has a Sanskrit name.

Listen to the salutation of the dawn,
Look to this day for it is life, the very life of life,

In its brief course lie all the verities and realities
> Of our existence.

The bliss of growth, the splendour of beauty,
For yesterday is but a dream and tomorrow
> Only a vision.
But today well spent makes every yesterday a
> Dream of happiness
And every tomorrow a vision of hope.

Look well therefore to this day,
Such is the salutation to the dawn.

Truly, this is the day that God has made and we can rejoice and be glad in it.

Let Go and Let God

My late father-in-law, Bill Somerville, was a scientist who, for some years, lectured in a college in Calcutta. During this period in his life he also studied theology, and his later books on Christianity brought evidence of his mind wrestling with issues of faith. In his book, *A First Introduction to the New Testament* he has an interesting way of interpreting the passage in the sixth chapter of Matthew's Gospel where Jesus exhorts his followers to 'take no thought for the morrow'.

He put it this way:

Sometimes this is translated, 'be not therefore anxious for the morrow'. The world would be chaotic if no one ever planned ahead. It may however, be right for some exceptional people not to take any thought for the morrow. Jesus may have intended this lesson for his disciples, who were to go out to spread abroad the message which he had entrusted to them. They were to travel from place to place, and there would always be people interested in their message and eager to give them hospitality. At the same time, 'Take no *undue* thought for the morrow' would apply to everyone. It is right to plan ahead, but to constantly be worrying over the future is wrong and can spoil a person's whole life.

William Somerville, A First Introduction to the New Testament

Much of our time is spent in planning for the future. Our days are filled with thoughts for the morrow. Often anxious ones. How do we come to a balance in this? How do we live with some thought for the future, but in such a way that our thinking does not ruin the preciousness of the present moment?

Part Eleven

Travelling Lightly and with Laughter

Lord of the unexpected,
bless our journeys
with lightness and laughter
on
these
paths
we never planned to take
but
through
your surprising Spirit
find
we
are
actually
on!

The Imaginative Weaver

Think for a moment of this beautiful image of God as 'the imaginative weaver' of our lives.

- Be still for a few minutes.
- Am I accepting of God's weaving in me?
- What new possibilities is God opening in my life?
- How do I respond to these?

David Perry, a Methodist minister, assists us in this meditation through the words of one of his prayers.

> O God, the imaginative weaver,
> take the thread of my life in your gentle hands
> and weave my love creatively,
> hopefully and purposefully,
> generously and graciously,
> into the fabric of this world's need.

> *David Perry, in* Cradle of Life,
> Methodist Prayer Handbook 2003–2004

The Coming of Dawn

> Death
> is
> not
> the
> extinguishing
> of
> the
> light.

It
is
putting
out
the
lamp
because
the
dawn
has
come.

Rabindranath Tagore, Collected Poems and Plays

When my late wife Dorothy was very young she was taken by her parents, who were at that time living and working in Calcutta, to watch the funeral procession of the great poet Tagore. On that day, millions of people of all cultures and faiths lined the streets of the city – all mourning the passing of one of their nation's noblest souls.

Tagore's memorable words transcend our often narrow religious traditions, and are timeless. They were written by an individual with a heart and mind permeated with grace, compassion and wisdom. One who had travelled deeply into the heart of the divine. In my own days of sorrow, I have been captured and comforted by his imagery of the lamp being put out because the dawn has come. Many centuries earlier, the mystic Kahil Gibran had expressed that reality another way when he said, 'And when the earth shall claim your limbs, then shall you truly dance.'

The belief that death is only a moment of transition and that wider possibilities lie ahead is a central tenet of the world's great religions. On our different, yet connected paths we all await the coming of the dawn.

Travelling without Fear

Lord, the earth is full of your constant love.

Psalm 119.64

May God write a message upon your heart,
Bless and direct you,
Then send you out
Living letters of the Word.

From This is the Day

The one supreme conviction that I cannot get away from
and – without any dramatics – am quite willing to die
for is that only the spiritual can mould any future worth
having for the world.

George MacLeod, founder of the Iona Community,
in This is the Day

Surprising God,
in these times
of terror,
of hidden fear;
of increasing uncertainty,
send an e-mail
with the news
that there is
ANOTHER WAY,
not of escape,
but of love –
where
awareness,
integrity of spirit,
generosity of heart

and
laughter
meet as companions,
celebrate their connection,
and transform
our hesitancy of spirit
for the
WHOLE EARTH
is
FULL OF YOUR GLORY
and we
ARE HELD IN THE PALM OF YOUR HAND.

On Being Busy!

JESUS IS COMING
LOOK BUSY

Words on a fridge magnet

Lord,
I love these fun words
on my friend's fridge door,
but
is it true
that I have to look busy
when you are around?

I'm always busy,
and I thought that at least
when you came,
there would be time to talk,
have a drink, relax,
and maybe watch the football.

For I once read
that when you were visiting
two sisters,
one of them just sat at your feet, lay back,
and did nothing but listen to your words.
And you told her that was OK.

So may be it's OK
to watch football together,
and have a beer
when you come round.
Let me know.
See you soon.

As Jesus and his disciples went on their way, he came to a village where a woman named Martha welcomed him in her home. She had a sister named Mary, who sat down at the feet of the Lord and listened to his teaching. Martha was upset over all the work she had to do, so she came and said, 'Lord, don't you care that my sister has left me to do all the work by myself? Tell her to come and help me!'

The Lord answered her, 'Martha, Martha! You are worried and troubled over so many things, but just one thing is needed. Mary has chosen the right thing, and it will not be taken away from her.'

Luke 10.38–41 (Good News Bible)

Being Single

None of us is so self-transparent as to know quite where, in fact, our hearts are set.

Nicholas Lash, The Beginning and End of Religion

Andrew is a writer and teacher and Carolyn is a minister. They worked for some years in Fiji, and have a great love for that country and its people. There are very few things in life which don't interest them, and they watch a lot more films than I do. We have shared many good times together and much laughter.

Dear Carolyn and Andrew

It was great to hear from you. Thanks for caring. It's over three years since Dorothy died, and I still find it difficult to think of myself as a 'single person'. I suppose that's not surprising having shared my life and work with Dorothy for twenty-seven years.

I remember reading somewhere that for all of us, no matter how strong an individual's partnership may be, we are essentially 'on our own' at many levels. I believe that's true, but what I miss (among hundreds of other things) in my single status is not having what I would describe as a living reference point, a compass, a place of focus, alongside your life day by day. I know from many of the letters I receive that others feel the same.

I may be wrong in this, but perhaps we all need a 'special other' – sharing our existence at a particular level to make us more human – more fully alive. I don't necessarily mean in a marriage relationship – that special other can be a soul-friend. And it's interesting how many people now are looking at the wisdom from the Celtic world which talks about soul-friends, companions in the Spirit.

On another issue, related to 'being single' – why do some folk (I am sure from kindly concern) ask you in a particular way which is almost impossible to describe, 'Is it not time that you were thinking about getting married again?' Do you think people in Palestine asked Jesus if he was going to get married? Anyway I have had some good fun when people ask me this, and if you can think of a reply which combines both fun and gratitude for them asking, pass it on!

Speak soon.

Peter

Jesus, you were single, so thanks for walking alongside the rest of us in the same state!

Food for a Pilgrim

Whether the main meal each day is at noon or in mid-afternoon, two cooked dishes on every table should be enough to all for the differences of taste so that those who feel unable to eat from one may be satisfied with the other.

Two other dishes, then, should be enough for the needs of all, but if there is a supply of fruit and fresh vegetables available a third may be added.

A full pound of bread every day for each member of the community should be enough both on days where there is only one meal and on those when there is supper as well as dinner.

If, however, the workload of the community is especially heavy it will be for the abbot or abbess at the time to decide whether it is right to make some addition to the amount of food available.

The same quantities should not be served to young children as to adults. They should receive less which will preserve in this, as in all monastic a practice, the principle of frugality.

We must always be careful to avoid excessive eating which might also cause indigestion. Nothing is so opposed to Christian values as overeating, as we can see from the words of our Lord: 'take care that your hearts are not weighed down with over-eating' (Luke 21.34).

From the Rule of Saint Benedict, in The Benedictine Handbook

> *Sustainer of life,*
> *At a time when many are hungry*
> *May I not be weighed-down*
> *Through over-eating!*

One Hundred Years On

Margaret is a close friend who is now 100. She has a shining faith in God and is a special person for many people. Despite her increasing frailty she is still interested in other people and in the world which has changed considerably since she first came into it in 1904.

Dear Margaret

Thanks for your phone call. I still can't believe that you will be 100 next week, but I'll certainly be there to celebrate with you and the others. I hope that there are lots of laughs, stupid jokes and some good wine! And food!

A couple of days ago one of our mutual friends said to me something which I must pass on. Irene was talking about how much she enjoyed visiting you and then said, 'Margaret has taught me so much about how to remain aware of the world and concerned for others right into great old age.' I echo these sentiments.

When I come to see you, I always come away feeling spiritually refreshed. I know that your body is very frail now, but you still have a real ministry of love to all your visitors. Perhaps it's your involvement in the lives of many others that has kept you so alive to life, and to God.

I don't expect you ever thought you would reach 100, but you have, and we have lots to be thankful for in that milestone. You are ready for death, but also for life. You know in whom you have trusted, and although you are so committed to Christ's way, you have never become overly pious or self-righteous. And you always have a twinkle in your eye, accepting human foibles!

You have asked me to say a prayer on your birthday. I will make it short. How does this sound?

> Today we give thanks for Margaret who still shows us all what it means to live in God's goodness and love every day.

See you soon. Don't do anything too outrageous before your birthday party.

Peter

Life is Stranger than Fiction

Sometimes life is stranger than fiction. Mystery can come in many shapes and sizes. One day when our home was in India, I had occasion to write to the local income tax officer. Even in a country where bureaucracy is often over the top, Mr Venkatraman's address must be something of a record-beater! Did everyone who contacted him by mail have to write all of this on the envelope? What if you were in a hurry? Or if your pen ran out? Was it a practical joke played on unsuspecting churchworkers from overseas? Would the letter reach him, if even one line of the address was missed out? Does everyone in India have a large envelope?

Anyway, here is his address if you ever want to contact him. (He may be retired – totally worn out from reading his mail!)

> Mr G. P. Venkatraman,
> Income Tax Officer,
> Madras Section,
> First Assessment Range,
> First Administration Division,
> Tamilnadu Charge,
> Income Tax Department,
> Ministry of Finance,
> Government of India,
> Ground Floor,
> Wanaparthy Palace,
> Central Revenue Building Campus,
> 121, Nungambakkam High Road,
> Numgambakkam,
> Madras, 600 034,
> Tamilnadu,
> INDIA

> *Lord, we thank you*
> *that we don't need*
> *a sixteen-line address*
> *for you to find us*
> *wherever we are*
> *in your world!*

A Free Holiday

The phone rang. The voice said, 'Congratulations. You have been selected for an amazing free holiday worth one thousand pounds, with all flights included.' Of course there was a catch. The possibility of a 'free holiday' was dependent on my allowing some firm of kitchen designers to revolutionize my perfectly adequate cooking space! You won't be surprised to know I never got the holiday.

> Do
> I
> Want it
> Lord?

> > Do
> > I
> > Need it
> > Lord?

> > A
> > FREE HOLIDAY
> > Worth
> >   One thousand pounds
> >   PLUS
> >   All flights.

I could have had it,
but I don't really want a new kitchen,
and come to think of it,
I don't need one,
even with a loose tile above the sink.

Do you understand, Lord?
for
everyone else thinks
I'm mad for
rejecting
TWO WEEKS IN THE SUN!

Dyeing Your Eyebrows

There is a single-line entry in the diary of Andy Warhol
and it reads:

I
HAD
A
LOT
OF DATES
BUT DECIDED
TO STAY
AT HOME
AND DYE
MY
EYEBROWS.

Andy Warhol (author's layout)

We may not dye our eyebrows, but I think most of us can
identify with Andy Warhol's diary entry. Out there are
various possibilities, but we chose another way. We go one
road, instead of another, and often have not the slightest
idea why we have made that particular choice!

Sometimes there are so many possibilities that we go
into a kind of paralysis – uncertain how to move forward.
Yet for millions in the world, there are actually very few
choices – a reality that came home to me many times when

working in India. For many village families, just to survive the day was a small miracle. To find enough food for the family and some water, and to be able to scratch a handful of rupees from somewhere took every ounce of energy and imagination.

I love the humour in Warhol's words, but they also make me realize how fortunate I am to be living in a part of the world where choice is possible.

Lord, when I am in a muddle, or unable to choose which way to act, can you please give me a little help, or a bit of calm!

One Precious Life

Dear Liz

In one of her poems Mary Oliver talks about the preciousness of life, and every time I read her words I come to a momentary standstill. We are precious and our lives are sacred, but how many of us actually live knowing it is true?

Recently I was in a small hospital in Palestine where profoundly disabled children and young people are cared for by an incredibly dedicated staff. Some of the children carry within their frail and often tiny bodies multiple disabilities. Many of them are at this centre because their parents have found it impossible to nurse them at home. Others are there because they have literally been abandoned.

The whole place is a work of love set in the midst of the spiralling violence which is evident everywhere in Palestine. For most of the staff even to get to work in the morning, through the various Israeli checkpoints, is a journey fraught with danger and mountains of frustration. To an outsider like myself, it seems almost impossible that the work in such a centre can continue at all given the intensity of the

Palestinian–Israeli conflict. Even during my visit I heard the sound of mortar several times.

When I was speaking to a young nurse in the centre, I asked her if she ever found it hard to work alongside such profoundly disabled children and teenagers. She paused for a moment and then quietly said, 'Not when I remember that every life here is a precious life.' I was almost in tears on hearing her reply. Here we were surrounded by young people facing huge health problems just to survive, in the middle of a town where death through violence is a daily reality, and here was this beautiful, young Palestinian woman reminding me about the ultimate preciousness of life. That in itself was a precious moment amid what I truly believe is sacred work.

In your own work with physically disabled young people, I know how much you respect the preciousness of each person. That is special. Your valuing of the individual shows me that it is still possible to celebrate our precious lives, even in a society where relationships can be fleeting and so much is disposable. And that is why it is so important to share the stories, not only those of terror and of war, but of where love triumphs.

Brother Roger of the Taizé Community in France once wrote a prayer about our preciousness in God's eyes. It comes with my love and appreciation for your work.

> O Christ, tirelessly you seek out those who seek you and think that you are far away; make us able, at every moment, to place our spirit in your hands. While we were still searching for you, already you had found us. However poor our prayer is, you hear us far more than we can imagine or believe.

The sun still shines, go gently . . .

Peter

The Hovering Spirit

Dear Rachel and Jack

At present I am in the Northern Territory of Australia. A place of the hovering spirit! Travelling under the bright evening stars in the stillness of this desert outback is to be in touch with something of that mystery which has been understood by Aboriginal people for over forty thousand years. Yes, forty thousand, and many scholars think a lot more than that!

Your own existence feels so temporary in this vast landscape, formed over tens of millions of years. Yet I also feel deeply at peace – held in nature's beauty and in its silent invitation. This extraordinary landscape reveals its truth through desert skies, flame-red rocks, ancient pathways and hidden springs filled with sweet water. It has a cosmology all of its own.

Throughout the millennia, Aboriginal people have developed an understanding of this cosmology – the natural forces of the earth, the inhabitant flora and fauna, indeed the total cosmos in which man, woman, animals and natural phenomena are linked. And today this vast canvas of knowledge, which was essential for human survival through the centuries, continues to be evoked in song, poetry, ceremony and in amazingly beautiful ritual painting. In fact I have just returned from spending a couple of hours with an Aboriginal elder who is also a fine painter.

As I try to take in these dimensions of knowledge I am more and more convinced that if humans are to survive into the future it will only be possible if they recover at least some awareness of their sacred interconnectedness with all that lives. It's not possible to do that in the same way as Australia's indigenous people, and it would be wrong to do so, yet in beginning to accept that we inhabit a sacred universe (and not one that can be constantly dominated by human greed) we awake to these paths of interdependence and interconnection.

Aboriginal spirituality is so grounded and practical. The Australian writer David Tacey wrote a book about emerging spiritualities within his own country. I was very attracted by its title – 'Re-enchantment'. In his book, David makes a strong plea for an earthed spirituality, and in reference to Aboriginal knowledge of the sacred says this:

> For Aboriginal people, the 'natural' way to live involves also a supernatural, mythological or imaginal dimension, and yet this supernatural dimension is eminently realistic, since it commands respect for the land, restrains human brutality, and urges us to relate to the environment with love, reverence and awe.

I think that is immensely helpful as we seek to discover a spirituality of connection with the natural order. In Christian thought we are sometimes starved of 'imaginal dimensions' in our attempts to connect theology and the good earth. Yet we need not be! It is hugely exciting that we can listen to cultures such as that of the Aboriginal people here in Australia, and in a certain sense be transformed by them, even if our understanding is limited. And if that sounds like a contradiction, then it is!

I am so grateful for this experience. The warm winds of the hovering spirit are truly opening my mind and heart. This silent inland has many songs!

Shalom.

Peter

Acknowledgements

'An African Creed', in Vincent J. Donovan, *Christianity Rediscovered: An epistle from the Masai* (SCM Press, London, 1978), p. 200.

Angie Andrews, 'There is precious little acceptance . . .', in Dorothy Millar, ed., *Seeds for the Morrow* (published privately, 2001).

Philip Andrews, 'The Song of the Magi', in Ron O'Grady and Lee Soojin, eds., *Suffering and Hope* (Christian Conference of Asia, Singapore, 1976).

Dietrich Bonhoeffer, *Letters and Papers from Prison* (Macmillan, 1954).

Ian Bradley, *Columba: Pilgrim and pentient* (Wild Goose Publications, Glasgow, 1996).

Anna Briggs, 'We lay our broken world', in *Songs of God's People* (Oxford University Press, 1988).

Ruth Burgess, 'The desert waits', in Janet Morley, ed., *Bread of Tomorrow* (SPCK/Christian Aid, London, 1992), p. 67.

Pat Burvil, *Shut Up and Pedal* (published privately, 2003).

Helder Camara, *A Thousand Reasons for Living* (Darton, Longman & Todd, London, 1981).

Carlo Carretto, *Summoned by Love* (Darton, Longman & Todd, London, 1977), pp. 75–6.

Pedro Casaldaliga, 'Misa Dos Quilombos', tr. Tony Graham.

Edward S. Curtis, *Native American Wisdom* (Running Press, Philadelphia, 1994).

Danu, 'Goodnight God . . .', in Elizabeth Roberts and Elias Amidon, eds., *Earth Prayers from Around the World: 365 prayers, poems, and invocations for honoring the earth* (HarperCollins, Sydney, 1991).

Jock Dalrymple, *Simple Prayer* (Darton, Longman & Todd, London, 1996).

Noel Davies, 'You saw that we were only human . . .', in Noel Davies, *Love Finds a Way* (Shekinah Creative Ministry Co-op, Thornleigh, Australia, 2000).

Charles Davis, *A Question of Conscience* (Hodder & Stoughton, London, 1967), p. 238.

Neil Douglas-Klotz, *Prayers of the Cosmos: Meditations on the Aramaic words of Jesus* (HarperCollins, London, 1994).

Paula Fairlie, in Maria Boulding, ed., *A Touch of God: Eight monastic journeys* (SPCK, London, 1982).

'Forgive each other . . .', quoted in Noel Davies, *Campfire of the Heart* (Shekinah Creative Ministry Co-op, Thornleigh, Australia, 1994).

Carole Forman, 'Antarctica', in Elizabeth Roberts and Elias Amidon, eds., *Earth Prayers from Around the World: 365 prayers, poems, and invocations for honoring the earth* (HarperCollins, Sydney, 1991).

Jenni Sophia Fuchs, in Neil Paynter, ed., *This is the Day: Readings and meditations from the Iona Community* (Wild Goose Publications, Glasgow, 2002).

Good News Bible published by The Bible Societies/HarperCollins Publishers Ltd UK © American Bible Society, 1966, 1971, 1976, 1992.

Joyce Gunn Cairns, in Dorothy and Peter Millar, eds., *Notes for a Pilgrim* (published privately).

Michael Hare Duke, ed., *Praying for Peace: Reflections on the Gulf crisis* (HarperCollins, London, 1991), p. 8.

Vaclav Havel, *Living in Truth* (Faber and Faber, London, 1987).

Herman Hesse, *Siddhartha*, tr. Hilda Rosner (New Directions, New York, 1951).

'I believe, O Lord . . .', in Esther de Waal, ed., *The Celtic Vision: Prayers and blessings from the Outer Hebrides* (Darton, Longman & Todd, London, 1988), p. 20.

Pope John Paul II, *Fides et Ratio* (Catholic Truth Society, London, 1998).

Kathy Keay, ed., *Laughter, Silence & Shouting: An anthology of women's prayers* (HarperCollins, London, 1994), p. 160.

Korean prayer, 'Like the seed . . .' ©?

Kosuke Koyama, *No Handle on the Cross: An Asian meditation on the crucified mind* (SCM Press, London, 1976).

Nicholas Lash, 'None of us . . .', in *The Beginning and End of Religion* (Cambridge University Press, 1996), p. 21.

'Lord of every nation . . .', in Neil Paynter, ed., *This is the Day: Readings and meditations from the Iona Community* (Wild Goose Publications, Glasgow, 2002).

Runa Mackay, 'A God of Justice and Mercy', in *Exile in Israel: A personal journey with Palestinians* (Wild Goose Publications, Glasgow, 1995).

George MacLeod, in *The Whole Earth Shall Cry Glory: Prayers from Iona* (Wild Goose Publications, Glasgow, 1985).

Joanna Macy, in Michael Hare Duke, ed., *Praying for Peace: Reflections on the Gulf crisis* (HarperCollins, London, 1991), p. 146. Slightly adapted by the author.

John Main, *The Joy of Being: Daily readings with John Main*, ed. Clare Hollward (Darton, Longman & Todd, London, 1987).

Jorge Maldonado, 'Sent by the Lord am I', in *Sent by the Lord: World church songs*, vol. 2 (Wild Goose Publications, Glasgow, 1991).

Hyllis Maris, 'I am a child . . .', in Dorothy Millar, ed., *Words of Meaning* (published privately, 2001).

'May God shield you . . .', in Esther de Waal, ed., *The Celtic Vision* (Darton, Longman & Todd, 1988).

Kate McIlhagga, 'Bless, O God . . .' © Donald McIlhagga.

Nick Midgley, 'On the first day . . .', in Donald Hilton, *Liturgy of Life* (National Christian Education Council, 1991).

Hanah Mikhail-Ashrawi, in Janet Morley, ed., *Companions of God: Praying for peace in the Holy Land* (Christian Aid, London, 1994).

Peter Millar, 'As I come to a peaceful awareness . . .', first published in Peter Millar, *Waymarks: Signposts to discovering God's presence in the world* (Canterbury Press, London, 2000).

Pablo Neruda, 'Keeping Quiet', in Pablo Neruda, *Extravagaria*, tr. Alastair Reed (Jonathan Cape, London, 1974).

New English Bible © Oxford University Press and Cambridge University Press 1961, 1970.

'O Christ there is no plant . . .', in *The Iona Community Worship Book* (Wild Goose Publications, Glasgow, 1991), p. 62.

'O God, we watch the news . . .' © Jan Sutch Pickard.

Neil Paynter, ed., *This is the Day: Readings and meditations from the Iona Community* (Wild Goose Publications, Glasgow, 2002).

David Perry, 'O God, the imaginative weaver . . .', in *Cradle of Life*, Methodist Prayer Handbook 2003–2004 (Methodist Publishing House, Peterborough, 2003).

Alison Phillips, in *Comment*, vol. 23, no. 5.

Prayers from the Mexican church and the Syrian church, in Wild Goose Worship Group, ed., *A Wee Worship Book* (Wild Goose Publications, Glasgow, 1989), p. 15.

Reflection from El Salvador, quoted in John Carden, ed., *A Procession of Prayers: Meditations and prayers from around the world* (Cassell, London/World Council of Churches, Geneva, 1998), p. 178.

Extract from the Rule of St Benedict, in *The Benedictine Handbook* (Canterbury Press, Norwich, 2003).

Irene Sayer, 'Creator God . . .', in *Cradle of Life*, Methodist Prayer Handbook 2003–2004 (Methodist Publishing House, Peterborough, 2003).

Roger Schutz, 'O Christ, tirelessly your seek . . .', in *Praying Together* (Mowbray, London, 1982).

Albert Schweitzer, *The Quest of the Historical Jesus* (A & C Black, London, 1910).

Joe Seremane, 'Lord, forgive . . .', in *Lifelines* (Christian Aid, 1987).

Rabbi M. Shapiro, *Tangents: Selected poems 1978–1988* (ENR Wordsmiths, Miami, 1988).

Govind Singh, in Barbara Greene and Victor Gollancz, eds., *God of a Hundred Names* (Victor Gollancz, London, 1985).

Peter Solness, *Tree Stories* (Chapter and Verse Press, Australia, 1999).

William Somerville, *A First Introduction to the New Testament* (Longmans, Green & Co., London and New York, 1950).

Jan Sutch Pickard, 'On a still December day . . .', in Jan Sutch Pickard, *Out of Iona: Words from a crossroads of the world* (Wild Goose Publications, Glasgow, 2003).

David Tacey, *Re-enchantment* (HarperCollins, London, 2000).

Rabindranath Tagore, 'Death is not . . .', in *Collected Poems and Plays* (Macmillan, London, 1935/1985).

Desmond Tutu, *The Rainbow People of God: South Africa's victory over apartheid* (Bantam Books, 1995), p. 113.

I. S. Tuwere, *Vanua: Towards a Fijian theology of place* (Institute of Pacific Studies, Suva, Fiji, 2002).